One Pan Nan

One-Pan Cooking for One-Pan Cleanup

Nan Kelley

On Deck Media

Copyright ©2015 by Nan Kelley

All Rights Reserved. No part of this book may be reproduced or utilized in any form or by any means, electronic or mechanical, including photocopying and recording, by any information storage and retrieval system, without permission in writing from the publisher.

ISBN 978-0-692-52116-8

First edition November 2015
Printed in South Korea

Excerpt from *Killing The Shadows* by Val McDermid used by permission.

Design and production by Cyndi Clark

On the back cover (top to bottom): Chicken Parmesan Lasagna, page 140 •
One Pan Chicken & Greens, page 158 • Charlie's Chocolate Bread Pudding, page 173

Front and back cover author photos by Marcia Eden
Photo Credits: Marcia Eden: pages 5, 15, 64 • Karen Dearing: pages 2, 10, 38-39, 153 • Charlie Kelley: pages 25, 31-32, 40, 43, 71, 74, 86, 88, 96, 111, 117, 124, 129, 135, 139-140, 148, 154, 176, 178, 184, 187, 195, 209, 213 (middle right) • Frank Desiderio: page 26 •
Tom Zaleski: pages 95, 144-145 • Joey Herro: pages 110-111, 121, 128, 155, 156-157, 162, 164-165, 176-177, 185, 202 • Howard Sumrall: page 115 • Amy McLemore: pages 117, 132 •
Tyler Blair: page 118 • Mark Mitchell: page 141 • Nicki DeCroce: page 186 •
Anne Kelley: pages 196, 206-207 • Donna Holcomb: page 197 • Donnie Beauchamp: page 223

ON DECK MEDIA
NASHVILLE, TENNESSEE

For Charlie—When I was Lucy in the kitchen,
covered in flour and crying in front of a failed falafel casserole,
you were Ricky, the rock I could lean on...
the true leader of the band.

Contents

Acknowledgements 9

Introduction 11

Appetizers 17

Breakfast, Brunch & Breads 37

Salads, Sandwiches, Soups & Stews 63

Lunch & Dinner 103

Desserts 167

About the Author 222

Acknowledgements

This book is not a solo effort. Many people in my world gave their time, talents, and recipes to bring it to life. Thank you to:

My family—the Sumralls, Kelleys, Holbrooks, Bridges, and Broomes, the many friends, neighbors, and roommates over the years for sharing your recipes with me.

My video recipe guests for not only sharing your recipes, but your time as well.

Momma, Miss Pat, and Clara for the random and often phone calls double checking spellings, servings, and sour cream size.

Kim, Sharon, and Anne for digging up and sharing old photos to help me tell the stories.

Photographers Marcia Eden and Karen Dearing for posing me in person and capturing it in the pictures throughout this book.

Cindy Rich and Michael McCall, who have done my hair and makeup for television for a long time, for lending your talents to this new venture.

Regina Wilson for the inspiration and backdrop of your beautiful garden.

Robert St. John for hiring me, teaching me, and inspiring me—both in the kitchen and the community.

Cyndi Clark for putting this all together beautifully and on time...even though I wasn't!

Petrice Beard for helping me navigate the waters of the production of this book.

My language experts, Molly Hendricks, Cindy Rose, and Jamison Rotch for help with editing and catching all of the out of place punctuation.

The lean and mean rotating OPN crew—ace cameramen Mark Mitchell, Joey Herro, and Tom Zaleski.

Author Val McDermid and Kiri Gillespie of Little, Brown Book Group for allowing me to quote a line from Val's book *Killing The Shadows*. Val's words helped sum up one of my favorite stories in this book.

John Alexander for sharing the vision and guiding the ship.

Brian and Selita Reichart and everyone in the Red Gold Tomatoes family. Their tomatoes are only bested by who they are themselves.

Lastly and most importantly, my husband Charlie. There is no book without you. The many hours you have given to this project—taste-testing, editing, proofreading, shooting video, editing video, writing music, photographing food, and taking your writing gift and finding my voice on paper through words. I am so blessed that you are my business partner, life partner, and my best friend. I love you.

Introduction

For the record, I am not a professional cook—most of us aren't—but I do consider myself a professional eater. Food is a big deal to me; ask anyone who knows me. When I get hungry, I get grumpy...no matter where I am. It might happen when I'm with Charlie at Lowe's. He thinks I use it as an excuse to stop looking at power tools and pressure washers. When I get hungry, I lose focus. It might happen on camera, when I can't remember what the name of the TV show is that we're shooting, even though I have hosted that show for ten years! Yes, when I'm hungry, Katie better bar the door. And bring a snack.

While sometimes I wonder if my DNA is made up of tiny strands of Chicken Tetrazzini, I know my genes are the descendants of some of the best cooks in Hattiesburg, Mississippi, or anywhere for that matter. Folks who have been doing it for decades, using traditions and techniques that go back for generations. My grandmother spoiled us rotten with her home cooking. Sunday dinner (that's lunch) at her house was set out like a smorgasbord. Everything had been perfectly seasoned, sautéed, stewed, and steamed and was ready to pile onto plates. From her chicken and dressing to eggplant casserole, with pound cake made from scratch and divinity for dessert... when the humidity was right of course. Being only ninety miles from New Orleans, Cajun and Creole food were big influences, too. I will still put my mother's red beans & rice up against any version of the same in all the restaurants in the French Quarter. My aunt and uncle, Jeanette and Jerry Holbrook, were longtime restaurant owners who specialized in southern-style home cooking. People lined up to get their fried chicken and cabbage with cornbread.

It wasn't just my family who fostered my love of great cooks and fine food. South Mississippi is ripe with culinary talent. My mother is a hairdresser of fifty years, and her clients frequently show their appreciation in the form of food, mostly in the dessert department. Pecan pies, chocolate chip cakes, date nut bars, and lemon squares were specialties of some of her customers, and I was the beneficiary of all that appreciation momma received for those cuts, colors, and updos.

Even my first jobs were in the food/restaurant world. I can't recall how young I was when I started working at Ward's on Hardy Street, but I can tell you that's where I learned to make a perfect soft serve swirl! I did a stint at Domino's Pizza after Ward's, and when I graduated from being behind the counter to waiting tables, I landed at the Purple Parrot Grill (now Crescent City Grill). The owner, Robert St. John, took a risk with an eater like me, hoping the food would make it from the kitchen to the customer without a detour to my mouth. I joke with him these days that I owe him money for all of the parmesan garlic bread I "quality assured" while I was suppose to be delivering it to tables.

To put it simply, food played a big role in my upbringing. It probably has as much to do with the people I was around and the memories made while enjoying all those meals as it does with the food itself. We all need food to live, but food was also about life. It was about conversation, comfort, family and friends, and heartaches and holidays. Whatever was going on in our lives, food was a part of it. It was and is the daily culture of my family. My mother talks about what we're going to have for lunch while we're having breakfast and whose homegrown green beans and squash have come in so we can pick some up for dinner.

The only downside to growing up around all those great cooks and all that good food is that I never really learned to cook myself. I never had to. All I had to do was show up at the dinner table. That tactic worked just fine while I was still at home, but when I moved to Nashville, I was on my own food wise, and those homemade meals went by the way side. I didn't starve, mind you, because ole grumpy will always find a meal, but it just wasn't the same. I continued waiting tables when I moved to Tennessee and was able to eat a crew meal after a shift, sometimes bringing home leftover food at the end of the night. I also worked as a singer, and fortunately, when you sing in a wedding band, the bride and groom, freshly baptized with wedded bliss, were always happy to have the band partake in their celebration. And, of course, fast food restaurants are as plentiful around Nashville as they are in most cities.

My dietary luck changed when I became roommates with Karen Dubel. She turned it all around for me. An excellent cook, Karen helped me get going in front of the stove. She said, "All you need are a few key recipes that you can lean on and a plan." She was right. Under her tutelage, I gained confidence in the kitchen, and before I knew it, Wendy and Ronald were calling saying, "Hey, we haven't seen you in awhile and just wanted to make sure you didn't need a cheeseburger or a frosty." Slowly, but surely, I was turning into a cook.

> *To put it simply, food played a big role in my upbringing. It probably has as much to do with the people I was around and the memories made while enjoying all those meals as it does with the food itself. We all need food to live, but food was also about life. It was about conversation, comfort, family and friends, and heartaches and holidays.*

One pivotal moment that tested my skills happened shortly after I met my future husband, Charlie. After dating for a while, it was time for me to meet his mom, Miss Pat. On one of her visits from Maryland, I invited her for dinner, and then I panicked. I had heard all about her wonderful cooking. What was I going to fix that would impress the mom of the man I was eventually going to marry? Karen was out of town at the time, so I called my friend Cindy Rose, and she gave me a recipe called Pork Chop Skillet. A simple, easy, one-pan dish that she said even I couldn't screw up, and luckily, I didn't. Not that my cooking ability was integral for Miss Pat's approval, but it didn't hurt!

Eventually, Charlie and I tied the knot, and married life brought on more cooking at home and less eating out in order to save money. With my newly found confidence in the kitchen, I started working on all of the dishes from my childhood—those yummy, southern casseroles. Now, Charlie grew up on a farm on the east coast in Maryland and was accustomed to a meat and 3 vegetables on his plate, and none of them touched. So when I served him those casseroles, he looked at the plate with its one square-shaped serving of what I thought was heaven and said, "What's this? What are you trying to do? Cook everything in one pan, Nan?" One Pan Nan was born.

INTRODUCTION   13

These days, time is a commodity in short supply. Most people are just like me and lead busy lives that don't always allow the time to orchestrate a multi-pan production. While I love those big meals and they should be celebrated, I always keep busy people like me in mind. And of course, the more pots and pans you need for a meal, the more pots and pans there are to clean up afterwards. Dishwashing is one chore I can do without—that's why I keep Charlie around. Seriously, the more I can cook in one pan and the quicker I can clean up afterwards, the more time I have to spend around the table with the people I love, creating more of those treasured memories.

The recipes in this book have been collected through the years. Some I've created myself through trial and error, and many are from family and old friends. In addition, I've made some new friends along the way by way of video. A part of the One Pan Nan vision is to shine the light on people in communities everywhere. Artists, business owners, protectors, helpers, healers, and everyday heroes. We may not read about them in our favorite news feeds, but our communities depend on them and wouldn't be the same without them. Plus, everyone has a favorite one-pan, easy to prepare dish—be it a casserole, a quick stir-fry, or a skillet sensation.

So, we're traveling the country to meet these people and learn their recipes. We talk about their lives, why they do what they do, and they show us how to make their favorite one-pan meals in the process. I've found that the best conversations always happen in the kitchen. After all, food ties us all together, and no matter what part of the world we're from or what we do for a living, all God's children gotta eat.

One Pan Nan is my mission to help you have more time around the table with the ones you love and less time over the sink cleaning up afterwards. I hope these recipes inspire you to cook more as they did me. I hope they give you confidence in the kitchen, like my friends Karen and Cindy gave me. Most of all, I thank you for bringing this book and me into your home. I'm honored to be a part of your culinary life!

Appetizers

Cream Cheese Shrimp Ball

MAKES 6 SERVINGS

This is my favorite "Miss Pat" appetizer. I love the simplicity of it—shrimp, cream cheese, and cocktail sauce. It always gets lots of compliments from people who've never had it before. If by chance there are ever any leftovers of this after a party or a family get-together, I admit to sometimes hiding it in the fridge so Charlie doesn't beat me to it…we both love it that much.

- 4 ounces small, frozen, precooked shrimp (thawed) or fresh cooked shrimp
- 1 (8-ounce) package cream cheese
- 1 jar cocktail sauce (I like the spicy version)

1. Tear shrimp into small pieces and pat dry with a paper towel.

2. On a piece of wax paper, combine cheese and shrimp with your hands. Shape mixture into a ball. Wrap shrimp ball in wax paper and chill until ready to serve.

3. Pour cocktail sauce over the ball and serve with crackers.

Nan's Notes: *Make sure to dry the shrimp pieces well, as this will help combine them with the cream cheese more easily. You can make this up ahead of time, and keep it in the refrigerator. When you're ready, pour on the cocktail sauce, lay out the crackers, and you're done.*

Chipped Beef Dip

MAKES 10 SERVINGS

This is a Kelley family favorite. I'd never had chipped beef growing up in Mississippi, but Miss Pat cooked a lot with it in Maryland. Creamed chipped beef on biscuits was a favorite wintertime breakfast on their farm. She prefers the Esskay brand out of Towson, Maryland, but unfortunately that brand hasn't made it to Tennessee yet.

So when her friend Dee from back home came to visit, she kindly brought with her all of the packages of Esskay chipped beef that her local grocery store had in stock. Miss Pat was thrilled, and we were thrilled because that meant she could keep cooking up this yummy dip.

- 1 (8-ounce) package cream cheese, softened
- 2 tablespoons milk
- 1 (2½-ounce) package chipped beef, chopped
- ¼ cup green bell pepper, chopped fine
- 2 tablespoons onion flakes
- ½ teaspoon garlic salt
- ¼ teaspoon black pepper
- ½ cup sour cream
- ½ cup chopped pecans
- 2 tablespoons butter

1. In a large bowl, combine cream cheese and milk. Stir in chipped beef, green pepper, onion, and seasonings. Mix well. Fold in sour cream. Place mixture in an 8-inch pie plate.

2. In a skillet, sauté pecans in butter and salt over medium heat for 2 to 3 minutes. Sprinkle pecans on top of pie plate.

3. Bake at 350° F for 20 minutes. Serve with buttered crackers.

Bacon, Tomato & Mushroom Dip

MAKES 6–8 SERVINGS

I'm an apps kind of gal. Not the Android/iPhone kind, but the food kind. Christmas Eve is one of my favorite meals, partly because of the Seafood Gumbo we always have, but also because it's the time I bring out my "A-list" of appetizers. I like to have plenty on hand, since folks arrive at different times from church, and we like to visit a bit before the meal. This one is good to have in your arsenal when you need a hearty appetizer to serve before an entrée that's on the lighter side.

6 slices bacon

½ pound mushrooms, chopped

2 medium garlic cloves, finely chopped

1 envelope onion soup mix

2 dashes of white pepper

1 (8-ounce) package cream cheese, softened

1 (8-ounce) container sour cream

1 Roma tomato, seeded and finely diced

Chopped parsley for garnish

1. In a medium skillet, cook bacon. Remove bacon when done and drain on paper towels. Crumble and set aside. Pour drippings from skillet, reserving 1 tablespoon.

2. Add mushrooms and garlic to drippings and cook over medium heat for about 5 minutes, stirring occasionally. Add onion soup mix, white pepper, and cream cheese.

3. Simmer, stirring constantly until cream cheese is melted. Stir in sour cream and bacon and heat through. Remove from heat and fold in diced tomatoes. Garnish with parsley. Serve with crackers.

Nan's Notes: *Serve this with celery or cucumber slices to lighten it up. This also makes a great stuffed mushroom filling.*

Creamy Pumpkin Dip

MAKES ABOUT 3 CUPS

Pumpkin is not just for pie. It's the perfect dip for fall, and this passed the discriminating sweet tooth of Mr. Kelley.

- 1 (8-ounce) package cream cheese, softened
- 1½ cups powdered sugar (may use less)
- 1 (15-ounce) can pure pumpkin
- 1 teaspoon pumpkin pie spice
- 1 teaspoon orange extract
- ½ teaspoon ground ginger
- 1 teaspoon vanilla extract

1. In a medium bowl, blend cream cheese and sugar with mixer for 2 minutes or until smooth. Add pumpkin, remaining ingredients, and blend thoroughly.

2. Chill for at least 2 hours or until ready to serve. Serve with gingersnap cookies and fresh apple or pear slices.

Nan's Notes: *You can serve this in a small, hollowed-out pumpkin with a variety of dipping options: cinnamon sugar graham crackers, gingersnaps, or Biscoff cookies, along with pears and apples. Spread it on banana nut or zucchini bread as a topping. To keep apple slices from turning brown in color, brush with a little fresh lemon juice.*

Olive Cheese Bites

MAKES 6–8 SERVINGS

I've never been an olive fan. Never cooked with them, never ate them by themselves, and just kind of ignored recipes or dishes that had olives in them. Charlie, on the other hand, loves them. So our dear friend Clara Ward brought these over to the house last year for his birthday.

Being raised a proper Southern girl, I needed to try one because declining would have been downright rude! So I braced my palate, grabbed one, and popped it in my mouth...and then I took another...and another. I couldn't stop eating them!

The combination of the salty olives with the buttery, cheesy dough is just perfect. These little delights made me change my tune about olives. These days when I make a batch, I whistle while I work.

- 4 ounces shredded Cheddar cheese
- 4 ounces butter, room temperature
- 1 cup flour
- ½ teaspoon paprika
- 24 medium-sized pimento stuffed olives, drained

1. In a large bowl, blend cheese with butter. Sift flour and paprika into cheese and butter mixture. Mix to form dough.

2. Take one teaspoon of dough and roll into a ball. Flatten in palm of hand and place one olive in center. Shape dough around olive, rolling back into a ball. Repeat with remaining dough and olives.

3. Bake on ungreased baking sheet at 400° F for 12 to 15 minutes. Serve hot with dip or ranch dressing.

Nan's Notes: *This is enough dough for about 24 medium-sized olives. If olives are on the small side, then use less dough for each. You want the ratio of olive to dough to be equal, so that one doesn't overpower the other. Sprinkle in a little cayenne pepper for some heat if you want. You can make these up ahead of time and freeze the bites—just pop them in the oven when you're ready to serve.*

Mexican Wontons

MAKES 28–30 WONTONS

We love our neighbors. Kim and Holley are always sharing goodies with us—homemade biscuits for the dogs, scarves to keep us warm on cool Nashville nights, and delicious food. When they learned I was working on a second book, Kim kindly offered up this recipe. The name alone won me over. It's two cultures colliding into one tasty little appetizer.

- 1 pound sausage, browned and drained (I like hot)
- 1 small bottle ranch dressing
- 2 cups freshly shredded Cheddar cheese
- 1 red pepper, diced
- 1 package unbaked wontons

1. Preheat oven to 350° F.

2. In a large bowl, mix together sausage, dressing, cheese, and pepper. Set aside.

3. Turn a mini muffin pan upside down and gently mold a wonton around each inverted muffin slot. Bake in oven upside down until wontons are just slightly brown. Remove pan from oven and remove wontons from the bottom. Flip pan over and tuck each wonton into a slot, right side up.

4. Fill each wonton with a little sausage mixture. Return to oven. Bake until brown and bubbly hot.

Nan's Notes: *Make sure to work quickly when removing the wontons from the bottom of the pan. As they cool, they become less pliable, so you want to tuck them inside the slots while they're still fairly warm. I always remove as much of the grease from the sausage as I can by laying it on some paper towels and then patting it on top with additional towels.*

Nixie's Cheese Straws

MAKES 10–12 SERVINGS

Sharon "Rae" Thomas has been my best friend since we were 13 years old. We grew up 3 houses apart in Hattiesburg, Mississippi. She knows everything about me, and she loves me just the same.

When we were little, I had stars in my eyes, and I always joked with Sharon saying she would be my "lady in waiting," not really knowing what that meant at all! Sharon had it all together. Not only could she cook, she could sew, as well and made a lot of her own clothes. I was chronically late in those days, so sometimes Sharon would come to the house early before school just to help me get out the door on time. I think she ironed my cheerleading uniform more times than I wore it! There wasn't anything she couldn't do and do well, and she still does. She's now a top-notch realtor here in Nashville.

Sharon and I cherished our grandmothers, and we both had the pleasure of knowing and being around each other's. She loved my Nannie Broome, I loved her Nixie, and this is Nixie's cheese straw recipe. As far back as I can remember, cheese straws have always been a part of a Mississippi social event. They may not have been invented in my home state, but the two sure go way back…just like Sharon and I.

1 stick butter

1 pound grated extra sharp Cheddar cheese, room temperature

2 cups flour

½ teaspoon cayenne pepper (may add more for spicier taste if desired)

1 teaspoon paprika

1 teaspoon Worcestershire sauce

1. In a large bowl, mix all ingredients together.
2. Press out with a cookie press with a star tip onto a cookie sheet, forming about a 3-inch straw.
3. Bake at 350° F for 18 minutes.

Cheese Puffs

MAKES 10–12 SERVINGS

In the many years I've been enjoying my mother-in-law's cooking, I'd never had these little jewels until recently. She brought them in one night, and I was stunned that there was something in her recipe repertoire that I had not tasted. Warm, little butter-and-cheese-coated hunks of bread—how can you go wrong? I will never miss an invited meal at Miss Pat's because gosh knows what other wonderful goodness she might reveal at the dinner table.

1 loaf unsliced bread, cut into 1-inch cubes
¼ cup butter
¼ cup shredded sharp Cheddar cheese
3 ounces cream cheese, softened
2 egg whites, beaten stiffly

1. Melt butter and cheese in top of a double boiler. Cool slightly and fold in egg whites.

2. Dip bread cubes in cheese mixture. Place on greased cookie sheet and put in refrigerator overnight. Bake at 400° F for about 8 to 10 minutes.

Nan's Notes: *You can make these up for later use. Instead of putting them in the refrigerator, put them in the freezer on the cookie sheet. Once they're frozen, store them in a plastic bag in the freezer until ready to use.*

Gorgonzola & Pear Puffs

MAKES 24 PUFFS

One of my favorite one-pan entrées in the book is Mushroom-Stuffed Ravioli Sauté (page 131) because of two flavors: pears and Gorgonzola cheese. I love those two together, so why not recreate the pairing in an appetizer?

- 1 tube refrigerated crescent rolls
- 2 fresh pears, sliced and cut into small chunks
- 4 ounces crumbled Gorgonzola cheese
- ¼ to ½ cup finely chopped walnuts

1. Unroll crescent dough into one long rectangle, sealing the seams and perforations. Cut into 24 pieces. Lightly press each piece into the bottom and up sides of an ungreased mini muffin pan.

2. Bake at 375° F for 3 minutes. Remove pan from oven. Place a couple of pear pieces in each cup and top with sprinkles of Gorgonzola cheese and walnuts. Bake 8 to 10 minutes or until cheese is melted. Serve warm.

Bruschetta

MAKES 6–8 SERVINGS

I've had the pleasure of hosting a fundraiser for the last couple of years in one of my favorite cities, Gatlinburg, Tennessee. It's called Taste of Autumn, and it raises money for the United Way of Sevier County by showcasing dishes from local restaurants. A chef from one of the restaurants served a variation of this bruschetta, and I just loved the flavor. It's the perfect appetizer for an Italian meal…or if you ask me, a meal in itself.

BALSAMIC GLAZE:

1 cup balsamic vinegar

BRUSCHETTA:

½ slender French baguette, cut into slices

Butter

Garlic powder

Pinch of salt

3 medium tomatoes, chopped

5 to 6 large fresh basil leaves, chopped

2 teaspoons Italian seasoning

2 tablespoons balsamic vinegar

1 tablespoon olive oil

Salt and pepper (to taste)

1 (4-ounce) container feta cheese

1. *Balsamic Glaze:* Pour balsamic vinegar into a small saucepan and bring to a boil. Reduce heat and simmer for about 30 to 40 minutes or until vinegar has reduced down to a syrupy consistency. Cool before serving. Vinegar will thicken more as it cools.

2. Preheat oven to 350° F. Place baguette slices on a cookie sheet and spread each one with butter. Sprinkle each with a little garlic powder and salt. Bake for 10 to 15 minutes. Remove from oven and cool completely.

3. In a small bowl, mix together tomatoes, basil (reserving some for garnish), Italian seasoning, balsamic vinegar, and olive oil. Stir to blend. Salt and pepper to taste. Place a spoonful of tomato mixture on each baguette slice and position slices on serving tray or platter.

4. Sprinkle each with a little feta cheese. Garnish with fresh basil and drizzle entire tray with Balsamic Glaze. Serve immediately.

Nan's Notes: *You can prepare everything in advance, but don't put this together until right before serving so that the crisp bread doesn't get soggy.*

Mixed Nuts Sauté

MAKES 1½ CUPS

I've never met a nut I didn't like...pecans, cashews, almonds, pistachios, all of them. This appetizer/snack recipe is one of my go-to favorites during the holidays. Here's how it came about.

Charlie and I went to a Kip Moore concert at the Franklin Theater just outside Nashville, and prior to the show, they served hors d'oeuvres in the lobby. One was a paper cup of mixed nuts with spices and herbs—a little heat, a little sweet, and delicious rosemary. So for Thanksgiving that year, in a decision that I literally made 30 minutes before the family was arriving for dinner, I took a shot at recreating them. Luckily, first time was a charm, and they were a big hit.

- 1½ cups premium mixed nuts
- 2 tablespoons brown sugar
- 1 tablespoon butter
- ½ to 1 teaspoon cayenne pepper
- 1 tablespoon rosemary leaves

1. In a large non-stick skillet, melt butter and toss in nuts. Stir to coat thoroughly, cooking for about 2 minutes.

2. Sprinkle brown sugar evenly on top and stir to coat. Add cayenne pepper (to taste) and rosemary and mix well. Cook for at least an additional 2 minutes to blend/meld flavors, stirring constantly. Cook longer for a crispier crunch.

Cranberry & Brie Stuffed Mushrooms

MAKES 12–18 MUSHROOMS

Stuffed mushrooms are a favorite of mine because they can hold all of the delicious, cheesy, dip-like ingredients that crackers or bread can—without the added calories! That's what I'm talking about. This is a wonderful option for the holidays with that hint of cranberry sauce.

- 2 tablespoons butter
- 12 to 18 baby portabella mushrooms, washed and stems removed
- 3 shallots, thinly sliced
- 2 to 3 tablespoons whole cranberry sauce
- 2 to 3 ounces Brie, rind removed and cut into small cubes
- ¼ cup finely chopped pecans

1. Preheat oven to 350° F. Melt the butter in a sauté pan. Add the portabella caps to the pan and cook for 1 minute on each side, over medium heat. Remove the mushrooms from the pan and place them stem side up in a small baking dish.

2. Add the shallots to the same pan and cook for about 5 to 7 minutes.

3. Spoon shallots into the mushroom caps. Add about a ½ teaspoon cranberry sauce to each of the caps, as well as one cube of Brie to each. Sprinkle pecans over the top of each.

4. Bake for 5 to 10 minutes, until Brie is bubbly and the mushrooms are cooked through. Remove from oven and serve warm.

Pesto & Brie Stuffed Mushrooms

MAKES 20–24 MUSHROOMS

These passed the Miss Pat test. I took these little gems to her birthday dinner, and they were a big hit, especially with her. I remember her calling me the next day to say how much she enjoyed them and that made me very happy!

- 1 pound mushrooms, cleaned and stems removed
- 1 tablespoon olive oil
- ¾ cup pesto, homemade (recipe on next page) or store-bought
- ¼ cup chopped, toasted pine nuts
- 4 ounces Brie cheese

1. Pour olive oil into a small bowl. Brush inside and outside of mushrooms with oil. Spoon 1 to 2 teaspoons pesto inside each mushroom and place stem side up in a baking dish. Drop a few pine nut pieces into each cap.

2. Top each with a small slice of Brie and broil in the oven until cheese is melted and golden brown on the top. Serve warm.

Pesto

MAKES ABOUT ½ CUP

Fresh basil, Parmesan, toasted garlic, and pine nuts with olive oil...nectar of the herb gods.

Basil is the big man on the herb campus. Just walking by my little herb garden and getting a whiff of sweet basil is aromatherapy that only Mother Nature could concoct. When the garden is full of basil, you have to cook with it, dry it, give some to your neighbors, and make lots of pesto!

There is something so cathartic and satisfying about whipping up your own pesto, the essence of many amazing Italian dishes. The flavor is so fresh, and if done right, you can taste every ingredient in it; one should not overpower the other.

- ¼ cup pine nuts, coarsely chopped
- 1 jumbo or 2 medium garlic cloves, sliced into several pieces
- 2 cups tightly-packed fresh basil, washed, dried, and loosely chopped
- ½ cup freshly grated Parmesan cheese
- 2 to 3 tablespoons olive oil (add more if needed)
- Salt and freshly ground black pepper to taste

1. In a dry nonstick skillet, toast pine nuts with garlic slices (skin still on) for a few minutes, being careful not to burn. Give the skillet a shake to stir and cook until slightly brown. Allow both to cool completely. Remove the garlic skin when cooled.

2. Add pine nuts and garlic to a food processor and pulse for 5 to 8 seconds. Don't overdo. Add in the basil and while pulsing, pour in ½ of the olive oil. Pulse for a few seconds. Pour in remaining olive oil and pulse until blended. Transfer pesto from food processor to a small mixing bowl and add cheese. Stir to mix. Taste and add salt and black pepper to taste. Cover tightly and refrigerate. If freezing, freeze without the cheese and add when ready to serve.

Nan's Notes: *Keep this in your fridge because you can make up a meal in no time. Grill a chicken breast, cook up some pasta, and plop some fresh pesto on top. Or slather on top of a thick piece of Italian bread for a snack. Use in soups and stews for great flavor.*

Breakfast, Brunch & Breads

Egg Muffins

MAKES 12 MUFFINS

I could eat eggs for breakfast every day, but I don't always have time to fix them...or time to clean up afterwards. This recipe was the answer for me. It's easy—you can make them the night before and get out the door in the morning with a great-tasting, protein-packed, egg breakfast to go.

6 eggs

½ cup milk

1 (3-ounce) package precooked real bacon (I like the pieces)

1 (4-ounce) can mushrooms, drained

Grated Cheddar cheese

TEX-MEX VERSION:

Instead of bacon, mushrooms and Cheddar cheese, use:

1 can diced green chilies

1 package Mexican blend grated cheese

Cumin

1. Grease a 12-cup muffin pan and preheat oven to 350° F. In a bowl with a pour spout, beat eggs, mix in milk, and add salt and pepper to taste. Stir well. Sprinkle a little bacon in each cup of muffin tin. Add a little cheese on top of the bacon and follow with a few mushrooms in each.

2. Pour egg mixture into each cup, filling almost to the top. Bake for 20 minutes or until egg is done and set in the middle. Cool for 2 minutes in the tin and then remove promptly to avoid moisture collecting in the bottom. Serve or store in refrigerator. Can be frozen.

3. From the refrigerator, reheat in microwave for about 20 seconds. From the freezer, microwave for about 1 to 1½ minutes.

Nan's Notes: *Make up your own combinations: Mediterranean with olives and feta cheese, Denver-style with onions, green peppers, and diced ham, etc.*

For toast cups

Miss Pat's Creamed Eggs

MAKES 4 SERVINGS

My mother-in-law Patricia Kelley is the kind of cook I want to be. She has shared so many recipes with me and really helped me look like a star in the kitchen.

Before she moved to Nashville, Charlie kept telling me about creamed this and creamed that, and I really didn't know what he was talking about. But I've since learned the creamed secret. Now I know how good creamed lima beans are and why Charlie will only eat peas if they're creamed…they're better that way!

Creamed eggs, however, really threw me, until I tried them. You can serve them for breakfast, lunch, or dinner, and if you're having brunch guests, you can dress them up in toast cups and make your company feel like royalty. A simple white cream sauce (or béchamel sauce) is the foundation, and if you're a fan of Eggs Benedict, you'll probably like this recipe, too.

2 tablespoons butter

3 tablespoons flour

2 cups milk

¼ cup shredded sharp Cheddar cheese

Splash of Worcestershire sauce

Salt and pepper to taste

4 hard-boiled eggs, peeled and thickly sliced

4 English muffins, split and toasted or 8 slices white bread, crust removed

Chopped parsley for garnish (optional)

1. In a heavy bottom saucepan, melt butter over medium heat and drop the flour in by the tablespoons. Mix constantly until blended and bubbling, about 2 minutes or so, without letting sauce brown. Add milk and stir to blend. Cook until sauce starts to thicken. Stir constantly to avoid clumping or sticking.

2. When sauce is thick, add cheese and a splash of Worcestershire sauce and stir. Salt and pepper to taste. Turn heat down and drop in egg slices. Gently fold eggs into sauce. Stir lightly to coat. Allow to heat through on warm.

3. *To serve with English muffins:* toast muffins on a baking sheet in the oven or in a toaster until golden brown. *For toast cups:* gently press bread slices into an ungreased muffin tin to form a little cup and bake at 350° F until toasty brown. Spoon creamed egg mixture atop English muffins or over toast cups. Sprinkle with chopped fresh parsley (optional) and serve hot.

Potato Sausage Casserole

MAKES 10–12 SERVINGS

I come from a long line of great cooks—my Aunt Tommie is one of them. I've had many good meals at her house down in Mississippi, and this one was no doubt on the menu. If you've got a big family, this is a big dish with big flavor!

- 2 pounds sausage, cooked
- 2½ cups grated Cheddar cheese
- 1 cup sour cream
- 1 (8-ounce) container French onion dip
- 1 (10¾-ounce) can cream of chicken soup
- 1½ cups chopped onions
- ¾ cup chopped red and green peppers
- 1 (30-ounce) package frozen hash brown potatoes

1. In a large bowl, combine sausage, cheese, sour cream, dip, soup, onions, peppers, and potatoes and mix well.
2. Pour into a large, greased casserole dish. Bake at 350° F for 1 hour.

Country Ham Quiche

MAKES 8 SERVINGS

This recipe is courtesy of a man who is very loved in East Tennessee, Chef Walter Lambert. I met him at the Taste of Autumn event in Gatlinburg where he was a judge for the local restaurant cook-off. When it comes to food, he knows what he's talking about.

An author of seven cookbooks, Chef Walter is Knoxville's Local 8 News chef and hosts the cooking segments on their noontime broadcast. He's a great educator too, and his book *Kinfolks and Custard Pie* is filled with country wisdom and stories, as well as delicious recipes. I was fortunate to be a guest on his show, and it was like going home. He's an easy, gentle spirit, and he always has a funny one-liner to toss out in the vein of those great country comedians we all know and love.

With Chef Walter on the Food City Kitchen set from WVLT's News at Noon

1 cup grated Cheddar cheese

1 cup chopped country ham

½ cup chopped onion

4 tablespoons plain flour

1 cup buttermilk

3 eggs

1 (9-inch) unbaked deep-dish pie shell

1. Place the cheese, ham, and onions in a bowl. Toss with flour.

2. Beat together milk and eggs and pour over ham mixture. Pour into pie shell and bake at 425° F for 10 minutes.

3. Reduce heat to 350° F and continue to bake for 30 to 35 minutes or until the quiche is puffed and brown. Serve hot or cold.

BREAKFAST, BRUNCH & BREADS

Breakfast Casserole

MAKES 8–10 SERVINGS

A lady who has fed me my entire life shared this one with me. And if I had to actually pay back my Aunt Jeanette and Uncle Jerry for all the meals they gave my poor college friends and me at their restaurant, I'd have to work three jobs and mow yards on the weekend!

Jerry's Fried Chicken was right by the University of Southern Mississippi campus in Hattiesburg. I would show up there with several hungry classmates in tow, and my aunt would wave us through the buffet line. Good food for budding, young minds of Hattiesburg.

7 slices loaf bread, cut up into small chunks

1 pound sausage, cooked (can be mild or spicy)

½ to 1 pound cooked smoked sausage or ham, chopped

7 eggs

1¼ cups milk

2 tablespoons yellow mustard

3 tablespoons Worcestershire sauce

3 cups grated Cheddar cheese

1. Lay bread pieces evenly along the bottom of a lightly greased 9½ x 11-inch baking pan. Sprinkle in cooked sausage and cooked smoked sausage or ham.

2. In a medium bowl, beat eggs and milk until smooth. Add mustard and Worcestershire sauce and blend well. Pour egg mixture evenly on top of casserole. Cover and refrigerate overnight.

3. Sprinkle cheese on top right before baking. Bake covered at 350° F for about 45 minutes to 1 hour. Serve hot.

Hindsight

I grew up right next door to my Aunt Jeanette and Uncle Jerry. Since they owned restaurants, they always had great leftovers in the fridge. The good stuff, too—fried chicken, beans & greens, cobblers of all varieties. You name it, and it was in their fridge. I would come home from school, walk through the chain link gate that separated our yards, and head inside their house to help myself. They never minded either. My family is just like that, and the adults love to see the kids eat. If Momma couldn't find me at home, all she had to do was holler out the window toward Aunt Jeanette's. I would holler back, "I can't talk right now, Momma. I'm too busy eating."

Some years later, I entered the Miss Hattiesburg pageant. I wouldn't say I was a tomboy growing up, but entering the pageant world, my attire had to change from jeans and T-shirts to evening gowns and heels. This pageant was a big deal because the winner moved on to the Miss Mississippi pageant and that meant scholarship opportunities. So, my whole family was in tow—Momma and Daddy, my sister Kim and brother Denny, and of course, Aunt Jeanette and Uncle Jerry were there too. After feeding me so much, they kind of took ownership of me as one of their own and rightfully so. Well, they brought their son too, my little cousin Kevin. Kevin was apparently shocked at what he saw when I walked out on the stage in my evening gown. Aunt Jeanette told me that he turned to her and said, "Gosh, Momma—look how pretty Nan looks. I never knew she looked like that. All I ever saw of her growing up was her backside sticking out of our fridge!" True story.

Cousin Kevin, Aunt Jeanette, and Uncle Jerry

Baked Apple Pancake

MAKES 6 SERVINGS

Griddle cakes, flap jacks, hot cakes, whatever you want to call them, I think they're better baked than griddled, flapped, or flipped. This says "Saturday mornings in the fall" like nothing else. Charlie feels loved when I make him pancakes, and he felt a whole lotta love with this one. Delicious!

- 1 large baking apple, cored and sliced thin
- ½ cup golden raisins
- 2½ tablespoons packed brown sugar
- ½ teaspoon ground cinnamon
- ½ teaspoon ground cardamom
- ¼ cup sliced almonds
- 4 eggs
- ⅔ cup milk
- ⅔ cup flour
- 2 tablespoons butter, melted
- Powdered sugar

1. Spray a 9-inch pie plate with nonstick cooking spray. Combine apple, raisins, brown sugar, cinnamon, cardamom, and almonds in a medium bowl and spread into pie plate.

2. Bake at 350° F for about 10 to 15 minutes or until slices start to soften a little. Remove pie plate from the oven and turn the temperature up to 450° F.

3. In a medium bowl, add eggs, milk, flour, and butter, mix well and pour evenly over apples. Bake for 15 minutes or until golden brown. Sprinkle with powdered sugar and serve.

Fresh Tomato & Basil Pie

MAKES 8 SERVINGS

I love the uncluttered flavor of this. Nothing fancy—just simple goodness. It's a delicious way to enjoy the bounty of your summer garden.

My little garden is just a few pots with some oregano, tomatoes, thyme, parsley, and of course sweet and purple basil. I love being able to walk out the front door, grab some fresh leaves, and walk back into the kitchen to use them. There is a sense of satisfaction that growing a garden brings, on top of having a fresh, homegrown flavor.

This is a warm version of my favorite salad, the caprese, starring my favorite herb, basil, and it's my favorite kind of cooking—says I, One Pan Nan!

4 to 5 ripe medium-sized tomatoes, sliced into ½-inch slices

Salt

1 (9-inch) refrigerated pie crust, room temperature

8 ounces freshly grated mozzarella cheese

¼ cup chopped fresh basil

¼ teaspoon black pepper

Salt

2 tablespoons extra virgin olive oil

Chopped fresh basil for garnish

1. Sprinkle each tomato slice with a little salt and drain in a colander for 30 minutes. Preheat oven to 400° F.

2. Sprinkle cheese into pie crust and spread evenly along the bottom. Layer basil evenly on top of cheese. Remove tomatoes from colander and pat each slice with a paper towel to remove any excess water. Place tomatoes on top of basil and cheese, forming a couple of layers as evenly as possible. Sprinkle pepper on top of tomatoes and add more salt if desired. Drizzle tomatoes with olive oil.

3. Bake 30 to 40 minutes. Garnish with fresh chopped basil. Cool before slicing, serving warm or at room temperature.

Nan's Notes: *You can put the pie under the broiler for a couple of minutes after it's done, browning the tomatoes to a nice hue. Perfect for brunch, Sunday lunch, or a light dinner.*

Nutmeg & Cinnamon Puffs

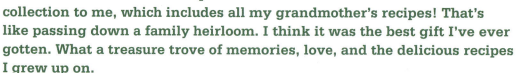

MAKES 12 PUFFS

I think my mother has finally taken me seriously as a cook. She recently handed down her entire recipe collection to me, which includes all my grandmother's recipes! That's like passing down a family heirloom. I think it was the best gift I've ever gotten. What a treasure trove of memories, love, and the delicious recipes I grew up on.

I stumbled across this one in this hallowed collection. These little gems sounded too good to be true, but indeed they are delightful puffs of cinnamony, sugary goodness that gave me that happy feeling of stopping by the donut shop on the way to Sunday school.

⅓ cup soft shortening

½ cup sugar

1 egg

1⅓ cups flour

1½ teaspoons baking powder

¼ teaspoon salt

1¼ teaspoons nutmeg

½ cup milk

TOPPING:

6 tablespoons butter, melted

½ cup sugar

1 teaspoon nutmeg

1 teaspoon cinnamon

1. In a medium bowl, blend shortening, sugar, and egg together thoroughly. Sift together flour, baking powder, salt, and nutmeg. Add in dry ingredients to wet mixture a little at a time, alternating with milk. Mix well. Batter will be thick. Using a spoon, drop dough into a greased muffin pan, filling each cup only about ½ way full. Dough makes just enough for 12 cups.

2. Bake at 350° F for about 25 minutes or until golden brown. Do not overbake. While baking, mix together the 3 dry ingredients for the topping. When puffs are done, remove from pan immediately. Dip puff tops into melted butter and roll tops in the cinnamon sugar mixture. Serve warm.

Cinnamon Swirl Bread

MAKES 1 LOAF

Is there anything better than hot bread straight out of the oven?

My friend David Howard is a potter in Gatlinburg, Tennessee. He creates many wonderful, useful, handmade pieces of pottery, including a bread baker. David includes a packet of quick bread recipes with each baker, and he let me share this one, Cinnamon Swirl Bread.

Perfect for weekends, Christmas morning while you're opening gifts, or a lazy Saturday morning with a little butter and a hot cup of coffee. You'll be proud to serve this bread and prouder to say you made it yourself.

- 2 cups self-rising flour, sifted
- ½ teaspoon cinnamon
- ⅔ cup sugar
- ¾ cup chopped nuts
- 2 eggs, slightly beaten
- 1 cup sour cream
- ½ cup butter, melted
- ¼ cup milk
- 2 tablespoons butter, melted
- ⅓ cup brown sugar
- 1½ tablespoons cinnamon

1. Combine flour, cinnamon, sugar, and nuts in a large bowl. Add in eggs, sour cream, butter, and milk, and mix well. Pour half of the batter into the well-greased bread baker or regular loaf pan.

2. Mix together melted butter, brown sugar, and remaining cinnamon in a small bowl. Swirl half of cinnamon mixture through the batter.

3. Pour remaining batter into bread baker and swirl the rest of the cinnamon mixture throughout. Bake at 350° F for 60 to 70 minutes. Make sure to put the bread baker in a cold oven and let it warm up slowly. No preheating is required, unless using a regular loaf pan.

BREAKFAST, BRUNCH & BREADS

Sour Cream Coffee Cake

I found this little treasure in Nannie's recipes—perfect for a lazy Saturday or Sunday morning with a hot cup of coffee and a clear schedule.

½ pound butter (2 sticks), softened

1 cup sugar

3 eggs, room temperature

8 ounces sour cream

2 cups flour

1 teaspoon baking soda

1 tablespoon baking powder

FILLING:

3 tablespoons melted butter

1¼ cups brown sugar

2 tablespoons flour

1 cup chopped pecans

1. Spray a 9 x 9-inch baking pan with cooking spray. In a large bowl, cream butter well with a mixer. Add in sugar and cream until fluffy. Add eggs and sour cream and blend.

2. Sift together flour, baking soda, and baking powder and add to butter/egg mixture. Blend well. Batter will be thick.

3. In a small bowl, mix together butter, brown sugar, flour, and pecans. With a spreader, spread ½ the batter into prepared pan. Sprinkle ½ filling on top of batter (I use my hands instead of a spoon), followed by remaining batter. Evenly sprinkle remaining filling on top.

4. Bake at 350° F for 45 minutes or until cake is set in the middle. Cool completely before serving.

Nan's Notes: *Make sure to use the correct size baking pan or you'll need to adjust cooking time and temperature. Also, as tempting as it is, let the cake cool completely before serving.*

BREAKFAST, BRUNCH & BREADS 53

Overnight Coffee Cake

MAKES 6–8 SERVINGS

This was in the family collection of recipes, and I believe it might be fairly old because it listed oleo, instead of butter or margarine, as an ingredient. The only place I see the word oleo these days is in crossword puzzles!

A lot of folks call this Monkey Bread, with many recipes calling for biscuit dough, but this is made with frozen rolls and has a glaze at the end. It's helpful on early, busy mornings—all you have to do is turn on the oven and start the coffee.

I made it recently for breakfast, and that night, Charlie ate the leftovers for dessert. Jerry, our little Boston terrier was really after it too. He always sits patiently and waits for a bite of people food, but when he got a whiff of this, he poured on his "look-how-cute-I-am-please-give-me-a-bite" routine. I think Jerry's got a sweet tooth like his daddy!

18 to 20 frozen rolls

½ stick butter, melted

½ cup brown sugar

1 (3-ounce) package vanilla pudding (not instant)

1 teaspoon cinnamon

½ cup chopped nuts

ICING:

½ stick butter, melted

¼ cup milk

Powdered sugar

Almond extract (to taste)

1. Spray a Bundt pan with nonstick cooking spray. Layer frozen rolls in pan and pour melted butter over rolls. In a small bowl, mix brown sugar and pudding mix together and sprinkle over buttered rolls. Sprinkle on cinnamon and drop in nuts. Place in a cold oven overnight.

2. Bake next morning at 350° F for about 30 to 40 minutes or until done. While baking, mix together icing ingredients in a small bowl. When coffee cake is done, turn out onto a cake plate. Drizzle icing over coffee cake while warm and serve.

Maple Syrup Strata

MAKES 6 SERVINGS

Strata is kind of the aristocratic name for casserole. It sounds so special and it is! The cream cheese element makes this one different and really tasty. I've made this many times, and it's become a favorite weekend breakfast treat at our house.

- 4 cups day-old French bread, cut into small cubes
- ½ cup golden raisins
- ¼ cup sliced almonds
- 4 ounces cream cheese, cut into ¼-inch cubes
- 3 eggs
- 1½ cups milk
- ½ cup maple syrup
- 1½ teaspoons vanilla
- 2 tablespoons sugar
- 1 teaspoon cinnamon
- Maple syrup for serving

1. Spray an 7 x 11-inch baking dish with nonstick spray. Put bread cubes in an even layer in dish. Drop in raisins, almonds, and cream cheese chunks evenly over bread.

2. In a medium bowl, beat the eggs well and pour in milk, maple syrup, and vanilla and blend well. Pour egg mixture over bread, cover, and refrigerate overnight.

3. Preheat oven to 350° F. Combine sugar and cinnamon in a small bowl and sprinkle evenly over dish. Bake 40 to 45 minutes or until knife inserted into center comes out clean. Serve with additional syrup.

Pecan French Toast Casserole

MAKES 6–8 SERVINGS

We have always been fortunate, no matter where we lived, to have wonderful neighbors, and our current neighbors are no exception. Holley and Kim are just a short walk through the trees, and they are both good cooks.

One weekend, Holley invited me over for a jewelry party brunch, the same day that momma and daddy were coming up to visit. Since it's a seven-hour drive to Nashville from Hattiesburg, I had plenty of time to attend, and this casserole was on the menu. I loved it and thought it would be a good one to make for my parents, so before I left, I asked her for the recipe. Before I could finish asking for it, she went to the fridge and pulled out an extra pan that she had already made up for me to take home and serve them. My parents loved it, too!

1 loaf day-old French bread, sliced 1-inch thin

6 large eggs

1½ cups whole milk

1 teaspoon vanilla

1½ cups half-and-half

⅛ teaspoon nutmeg

1 teaspoon cinnamon

TOPPING:

½ cup butter, softened

1 cup dark brown sugar, packed

1 cup chopped pecans

2 tablespoons maple syrup

1. Spray a 9 x 13-inch baking dish with nonstick cooking spray. Lay slices of French bread along the bottom.

2. In a large bowl, mix remaining ingredients together and pour over slices. Cover and refrigerate overnight.

3. In a small bowl, mix together topping ingredients with hands. Sprinkle the topping in chunks on top of casserole. Bake at 350° F for about 45 minutes or until set.

Nan's Notes: *Let the casserole bake for about 10 minutes, and then spread the topping around with a knife to cover the whole casserole.*

Cranberry Scones

MAKES 8 SCONES

What wins out when I'm face-to-face with a bakery display, and the elusive chocolate éclair is not on the scene? The scone. Hands down. Love them and love all kinds.

My friend Clara Ward gave me this recipe, and it's a great one. Scones are of course a good baked breakfast item, but they're also good in the afternoon or as a dessert. Great with coffee, or try them with a cup of black tea with cream and sugar. You just might feel like you're at Buckingham Palace.

- ⅔ cup buttermilk or plain yogurt
- 1 large egg
- 3 cups flour
- 4 teaspoons baking powder
- ½ teaspoon baking soda
- ½ teaspoon salt
- 8 tablespoons (1 stick) cold, unsalted butter, cut up
- 1½ cups fresh or frozen cranberries
- ½ cup sugar
- 1 teaspoon freshly grated lemon peel (optional)
- ¼ cup finely chopped pecans
- 1 tablespoon butter, room temperature

1. Heat oven to 375° F. In a small bowl, blend buttermilk and egg with a whisk. In a large bowl, put flour, baking powder, baking soda, and salt and stir to mix well. Add the butter and cut in with a pastry blender or fork until the mixture is crumbly.

2. Add cranberries, sugar, lemon peel, and pecans and stir to blend. Pour in the buttermilk mixture and stir until a soft dough starts to come together. Turn dough out onto a lightly floured surface and knead just until well-mixed. Shape dough into a ball and cut ball into 8 equally-sized wedges. Place wedges on an ungreased baking sheet and bake 20 to 25 minutes or until medium brown. Transfer to racks for cooling and spread a little of the soft butter on top of each. Cool completely before serving.

Nan's Notes: *Stash some fresh cranberries away in the freezer for those times of the year when they aren't available.*

Peanut Butter & Chocolate Chip Scones

MAKES 8 SCONES

As a Mississippi girl, it's not surprising that I love scones because they're a close kin to a southern staple, the biscuit. Plus, they're really easy to make. You don't need to let the dough rise, you don't need a mixer, you can put them together quickly, and you can add in whatever you like—blueberries, currants, cranberries.

Scones can be savory or sweet, and the British typically like them plain at teatime, served with clotted cream and jam. I like them with peanut butter and chocolate these days! This one can definitely be a dessert, too. Pop one in the microwave to warm it up, and serve it with a scoop of ice cream.

1 (5.33-ounce) can evaporated milk

1 egg

½ cup crunchy peanut butter (natural)

2 cups flour

3 teaspoons baking powder

3 tablespoons sugar

¼ teaspoon salt

½ stick cold butter, cut into small pieces

¾ cup chocolate chips

GLAZE:

1 tablespoon crunchy peanut butter (natural)

1 cup powdered sugar

1 to 2 tablespoons milk

1. In a small mixing bowl, add milk, egg, and peanut butter and whisk until peanut butter is smooth. In a large mixing bowl, mix flour, baking powder, sugar, and salt. Set aside.

2. Drop in butter pieces to the flour mixture and using a pastry cutter or a fork, cut in the butter until crumbly. This will take a couple of minutes. Add peanut butter mixture to the large bowl and mix with a spatula. Sprinkle in chocolate chips and mix until incorporated and dough starts to form. Transfer dough and any floury bits to a well-floured flat surface and knead gently 5 or 6 times to form dough.

3. Press dough ball out to form a circle of about the size of a 9-inch cake pan, about 1-inch thick. Cut dough circle into 8 wedge-shaped pieces. Lay each piece on an ungreased cookie sheet and bake at 400° F for 10 minutes or until golden brown. Do not overbake. Remove from cookie sheet immediately and cool on rack.

4. *Glaze:* In a small bowl, blend peanut butter, sugar, and milk. Drizzle desired amount onto each warm scone and serve.

BREAKFAST, BRUNCH & BREADS 61

Salads, Sandwiches, Soups & Stews

Watermelon Arugula Salad

MAKES 4 SERVINGS

One of our favorite restaurants in Nashville is Caffé Nonna in the Sylvan Park neighborhood. It's a cozy, Nashville original with delicious Italian food. We had their salad special one night, made with local ingredients and the sweetest watermelon ever! I came home and put my spin on it. It's so pretty on the plate and a refreshing way to enjoy summer's sweetest sensation.

- 4 loosely packed cups baby arugula leaves, ends trimmed
- 4 tablespoons crumbled feta cheese
- 4 teaspoons chopped fresh mint leaves
- ¼ cup coarsely chopped walnuts, toasted
- 1 small watermelon, about 25-inches in diameter and chilled
- Olive oil
- Balsamic Glaze (recipe page 30)

1. Place 1 cup arugula on each of 4 salad plates. Sprinkle 1 tablespoon feta and 1 teaspoon mint on each and top each with a handful of toasted walnuts. Drizzle salad with a little olive oil.

2. Slice watermelon in half. Cut 4 slices, about 1-inch thick. Quarter each slice into 4 equal wedge-shaped pieces and place all four pieces on top of salad on each plate, with points facing inward to form a pinwheel. Drizzle entire plate with Balsamic Glaze.

Mandarin Orange Salad

MAKES 4–6 SERVINGS

This one is from the kitchen of my one of my best college buddies and my very first roommate, Belinda Hicks Haeusler. We lived in a little apartment close to the campus of the University of Southern Mississippi, and I think we lived off this salad for weeks at a time. I didn't really do any cooking back then, so this recipe was like manna from heaven for me because even I could whip it up without any difficulty.

- 1 (16-ounce) pint cottage cheese
- 1 (3-ounce) box orange gelatin
- 1 (12-ounce) container whipped topping
- 1 (11-ounce) can mandarin oranges, drained

1. In a medium bowl, mix cottage cheese and gelatin very well.
2. Fold in whipped topping and mandarin oranges. Refrigerate for 30 minutes.

Strawberry & Pineapple Congealed Salad

MAKES 6–8 SERVINGS

I don't know if it's only a Southern thing, but we had a congealed salad at just about every Sunday dinner or formal meal. I forgot how much I loved them until I found so many congealed salad recipes in my mother's and grandmother's collections. This is one in particular I remember having all the time.

- 1 large or 2 small boxes raspberry gelatin
- 1 (8-ounce) can crushed pineapple, drained (reserve juice)
- 1 (21-ounce) strawberry pie filling

TOPPING:

- 1 (8-ounce) package cream cheese, softened
- 1 cup sour cream
- ½ cup sugar
- 1 teaspoon vanilla extract
- ½ to 1 cup chopped pecans

1. In a large bowl, dissolve gelatin in 1 cup boiling water. Add pineapple and stir. Add water to reserved juice to make 1 cup and pour into gelatin/pineapple mixture.

2. Blend in pie filling and stir well. Pour into a flat serving dish and refrigerate until set.

3. When ready to serve, combine cream cheese, sour cream, sugar, and vanilla in a small bowl. Spread on top of salad and sprinkle with pecans. Serve cold.

Nan's Notes: *Congealed salads are hybrids—serve at brunch with a quiche, at lunch with a sandwich, or as a side salad with dinner. My nannie served this on top of a nice green or butter leaf lettuce.*

SALADS, SANDWICHES, SOUPS & STEWS

BLT Pasta Salad

MAKES 4–6 SERVINGS

Sometimes you forget just how good a classic BLT is. So many times we try to take a simple idea and ramp it up with exotic ingredients or expensive cuts of meat, forgetting that sometimes simple is…well, simply better!

- 1 (10-ounce) package cheese-filled tortellini
- ¼ cup mayonnaise
- ¼ cup sour cream
- 1 teaspoon garlic powder
- 3 heaping tablespoons chopped fresh basil
- Salt and freshly ground black pepper to taste
- 3 tablespoons bacon bits
- 3 cups loosely packed baby spinach
- 1 pint grape tomatoes, sliced in half

1. Cook pasta according to directions. While pasta is cooking, mix mayonnaise, sour cream, garlic powder, basil, and 2 tablespoons of bacon bits in a large bowl. Add salt and pepper to taste.

2. When pasta is done, drain, put in bowl with mayonnaise mixture while pasta is still hot, and mix gently. Refrigerate for 30 minutes.

3. Fold in spinach and tomatoes. Sprinkle remaining bacon on top and serve.

Nan's Notes: *Add a little more mayo if you want. I'm always about a little more mayo!*

Sesame Cabbage Salad

MAKES 10–14 SERVINGS

This recipe is from a great cook who brought me out of my "I can't cook" shell. My friend and former Nashville roommate, Karen Dubel convinced me that I could cook if I tried. She saw potential in me way back then! She spent time teaching me while we fixed dinner together after work. She gave me the confidence I needed to start cooking for myself.

I still have all of the recipe cards she wrote out for me, and they are well-worn. Karen now lives in California with her husband and three beautiful girls and is no doubt still cooking up a storm.

- 2 (3-ounce) packages ramen noodle soup, crushed (I use Top Ramen's oriental flavor)
- 8 tablespoons sesame seeds
- 8 tablespoons slivered almonds
- 1 head cabbage, sliced thin
- 8 green onions, finely chopped

DRESSING:
- 6 tablespoons rice vinegar
- 4 tablespoons sugar
- 1 cup oil
- 1 teaspoon salt
- 1 teaspoon black pepper

1. In a hot, nonstick skillet with no oil, brown noodles, sesame seeds, and almonds separately. Set aside and let cool.

2. In a large bowl, mix together cabbage and onions and add in cooled noodles, seeds, and almonds 15 minutes before serving.

3. In a small bowl, mix dressing ingredients together and pour into noodle mixture. Toss gently. May add cooked chicken or ham that has been chopped into bite-sized pieces.

Nan's Notes: *This is a wonderful picnic dish. It makes a big portion so you can feed a lot of folks.*

Cilantro Salmon with Corn & Black Bean Salad

MAKES 2–4 SERVINGS

Charlie and I lived next door to Cliff and Clara Ward for ten years here in Nashville. The side doors of our houses were ten yards apart. If I had a problem when Charlie was out on the road or I needed anything, help was only a few steps away. Though we don't live right next door anymore, they are still an important part of our lives, and they are family to us. Clara is a heck of a cook. She's helped me so many times with ideas and recipes—many of them in this book. This is her Corn & Black Bean Salad recipe, and it makes a great summertime meal.

- 2 cans black beans, drained and rinsed
- 2 cans shoepeg corn, drained
- ½ cup fresh chopped cilantro
- 1 to 2 fresh jalapeños, seeded and chopped
- 4 scallions, chopped
- ¼ cup red wine vinegar
- ¼ cup olive oil
- 1 teaspoon Dijon mustard
- 1 teaspoon cumin
- 1 teaspoon salt
- ½ teaspoon black pepper
- 2 pieces skinless salmon fillets
- Sea salt and freshly ground black pepper
- Canola or vegetable oil
- Cilantro & Yogurt Dressing (recipe on next page)
- Cherry tomatoes and cilantro sprigs (for garnish)

1. Pour black beans, corn, cilantro, jalapeños, and scallions in a large bowl. In a small bowl, whisk together vinegar, olive oil, mustard, cumin, salt and pepper. Pour over black bean and corn mixture and gently toss. Chill in fridge for 30 minutes.

2. Wash the salmon fillets and pat dry with a paper towel. Sprinkle each side with sea salt, pressing salt into the fish, and then season with pepper. Heat a medium sauté pan over medium heat and pour in enough canola oil to cover the bottom. Lay fillets in the skillet and cook each side for about 4 to 5 minutes, flipping only once. Remove when done and drain on paper towels.

3. Put a generous amount of salad onto plate and lay salmon fillet on top. Drizzle dressing on top of salmon (to taste). Garnish plate with sliced cherry tomatoes and cilantro sprigs and serve.

CILANTRO & YOGURT DRESSING:

1 cup fresh cilantro, stems removed

½ cup plain yogurt

2 cloves garlic, roasted and skin removed

Juice of 1 lime

Dash of salt

1 teaspoon sugar

¼ cup olive oil

2 tablespoons apple cider vinegar

1. Place cilantro, yogurt, garlic, lime juice, salt, and sugar in the bowl of a food processor.

2. Pulse to blend well. While pulsing, add olive oil and vinegar in a slow stream. Refrigerate until needed.

Nan's Notes: *I added the salmon, but you can serve it with another type of fish or chicken, enjoy it by itself, or as a side dish.*

Pimento Cheese

MAKES 6 SERVINGS

There is nothing more Southern than pimento cheese. Like the deviled egg, it's a staple in every Southerner's diet, and I'm no exception. Whenever I start talking with my momma about making a trip home to Mississippi, she starts planning what we're going to eat. She says, "Now, I know you're going to be driving in here late, so I'll make up some pimento cheese so you can have it when you get in." My momma believes there is no food available between Nashville and Hattiesburg. I always pick on her about that, and she always threatens not to cook for me anymore, so I shut up real quick!

This recipe is a nod to several important influences: my mom because she always adds a little garlic powder, my friend Clara because she adds some cream cheese to her recipe, and Charlie because he wanted the pecans in there. My contribution is the jalapeño because I love that kick of heat. Hope you enjoy an updated twist to a loved classic.

- 1 pound block extra sharp (or sharp) Cheddar cheese
- ½ cup mayonnaise
- 2 ounces cream cheese, softened
- 1 jar pimentos, drained and chopped (reserve juice)
- ½ cup chopped pecans
- 2 heaping tablespoons chopped fresh jalapeño pepper (may add more to taste)
- Garlic powder to taste
- Salt and freshly ground black pepper to taste

1. Grate cheese block over a large bowl. Mix in mayonnaise and cream cheese (may add more cream cheese if creamier consistency is desired). Pour in a little bit of pimento juice if needed to aid in blending. Stir with a fork to blend.

2. Add pimentos, pecans, peppers, and garlic powder and mix well. Add salt and pepper to taste.

Nan's Notes: *Serve on bread as a sandwich, with celery sticks, crackers…or do like I do, and eat it straight out of the bowl with some corn chips.*

SALADS, SANDWICHES, SOUPS & STEWS

Miss Pat's Open-Faced Tomato Sandwich

MAKES DESIRED AMOUNT OF SERVINGS

My mother-in-law, Miss Pat, served this for lunch to the guys who worked on the farm where Charlie grew up. It was a big hit with them back then, and it's still a family favorite. Easy to make and even easier to eat.

English muffins
Mayonnaise
Basil, chopped
Tomatoes, sliced
Bacon bits
Salt and freshly ground black pepper to taste
Provolone cheese slices

1. Split muffin open and broil for a few minutes under broiler until lightly toasted.

2. Remove from oven and top each half with mayonnaise, basil, and sliced tomatoes. Sprinkle with bacon bits and salt and pepper to taste. Add a slice of provolone cheese to each half and return to oven. Broil until cheese is melted and bubbly light brown.

Nan's notes: *You can cook bacon slices and crumble them onto the sandwich or use real pre-packaged bacon bits. I added the basil for that little bit of fresh zing, but it's good without it as well.*

Edamame & Lentils

MAKES 6 SERVINGS

I didn't grow up with polenta, never even really heard of it until my sister-in-law Anne gave me this recipe years ago. While visiting her in Ohio before she moved to Tennessee, she gave me a stack of handwritten recipes on little pink cards, and this dish was on one of them. When I finally tried it, I realized that polenta is actually similar to the grits I grew up eating for breakfast. I guess if you're going to have grits for dinner, they should have a slightly fancier name!

- 1 (14½-ounce) can vegetable broth
- 1 cup water
- 1 tablespoon olive oil
- 1 cup dry lentils
- 1 (12-ounce) bag frozen edamame
- 1 medium green bell pepper, chopped
- 1 medium red bell pepper, chopped
- ½ cup chopped onion
- 2 tablespoons Italian seasoning
- 1 teaspoon salt
- 2 medium tomatoes, chopped
- Salt and freshly ground black pepper to taste
- Hot cooked polenta

1. In a slow cooker, combine broth, water, olive oil, dry lentils, edamame, peppers, onion, Italian seasoning, and salt. Cover and cook on medium-high for 2 to 3 hours or low for about 5 to 7 hours or until beans are soft and most of the liquid has evaporated. May add more water if needed.

2. When beans are done, stir in chopped tomatoes and turn slow cooker off.

3. Season beans with salt and pepper to taste and serve over prepared polenta.

Nan's Notes: *This is a good vegetarian choice for a no-meat night.*

Sausage Bean Soup

MAKES 4 SERVINGS

Give me a hot bowl of soup beside a crackling fire on a winter's night, and I'm a happy girl.

½ pound sausage

1 medium onion, chopped

1 (15½-ounce) can kidney beans, undrained

1 (14½-ounce) can diced tomatoes, undrained

1 pint water

1 bay leaf

¾ teaspoon seasoned salt

¼ teaspoon garlic powder

¼ teaspoon dried thyme

¼ teaspoon black pepper

½ cup chopped green pepper

1 medium potato, peeled and diced (approximately 1 cup)

1. Brown sausage and onion in a large saucepan, stirring to crumble meat. When meat is done, drain off drippings. Stir in beans, tomatoes, water, bay leaf, and seasonings. Cover and simmer for one hour on low heat.

2. Add green pepper and potatoes. Cover and simmer for 20 minutes or until potatoes are tender. Remove bay leaf before serving.

Paprika Potatoes & Sausage Soup

MAKES 6 SERVINGS

Love this soup! It's very filling, and all of the flavors work so well together. If you're on a budget, this makes a lot of soup so you've got dinner and plenty of leftovers.

- **6 chicken bouillon cubes**
- **2½ cups chopped onion**
- **2 tablespoons paprika**
- **4 potatoes, peeled and cut into ½-inch cubes (approximately 5 cups)**
- **1 pound green cabbage, coarsely shredded (approximately 8 cups)**
- **8 ounces kielbasa, coarsely chopped**
- **1 (14½-ounce) can stewed tomatoes**
- **½ cup sour cream**

1. In a 4- to 5-quart pot, bring 7 cups water, bouillon cubes, onion, and paprika to a boil, stirring to dissolve cubes.

2. Add potatoes and cabbage and return to a boil. Reduce heat and simmer 20 minutes or until vegetables are tender.

3. Add in kielbasa and tomatoes and increase heat to medium-high. Cook for about 5 additional minutes. Remove pan from heat and add in sour cream. Stir to mix and serve.

Italian Vegetable Soup

MAKES 6 SERVINGS

There's nothing better than walking into the house after working all day to the smell of dinner that's already done! Charlie and I had this for supper not too long ago, and we both went back for seconds. This hits the spot on a cool, fall night. Another good one from my sister-in-law Anne.

3 (14½-ounce) cans vegetable broth

1 (28-ounce) can crushed tomatoes, undrained

3 medium carrots, sliced

3 small zucchini, cut into ½-inch slices

1 medium yellow bell pepper, cut into ½-inch pieces

1 medium red bell pepper, cut into ½-inch pieces

½ cup chopped onions

2 garlic cloves, minced

2 cups shredded cabbage

2 teaspoons dried marjoram leaves

2 teaspoons oregano

1 teaspoon salt

¼ teaspoon black pepper

1 cup uncooked instant rice

½ cup chopped fresh basil

Freshly grated Parmesan cheese for garnish

1. Mix all ingredients, except rice and basil, in a slow cooker. Cover and cook on high for 3 to 4 hours or low for 6 to 8 hours or until vegetables are tender.

2. Stir in rice. Cover and cook on low for about 15 minutes or until rice is tender. Stir in basil. Top each serving with Parmesan cheese.

Nan's Notes: *You can use chicken or beef broth in place of the vegetable broth if you want. The fresh basil is a must in this one; make sure to stir it in last.*

Gloria's Vegetable Beef Soup

MAKES 6–8 SERVINGS

This is my momma's vegetable soup. When we had soup growing up at my house, 95 percent of the time it was this. And 100 percent of the time, there were no leftovers!

1 pound beef stew meat

Soup bone (optional)

1 large onion, chopped

2 small potatoes, peeled and chopped

¼ to ½ bag frozen baby lima beans

¼ package spaghetti, broken into 3-inch pieces

1 large bag frozen vegetables for soup

2 carrots, peeled and sliced

½ bag frozen green peas

2 celery stalks, chopped

1 (14½-ounce) can diced tomatoes, undrained

1 (8-ounce) can tomato sauce

1 can white shoepeg corn, drained

1 cup frozen cut green beans

1 cup frozen cut okra

Salt and freshly ground black pepper to taste

1. Place stew meat, soup bone, and onion in a large stockpot and cover with water. Cook on medium until meat is a little tender.

2. Add potatoes, lima beans, and spaghetti and cook for about 15 to 20 minutes, adding more hot water if needed.

3. Add frozen vegetable bag, carrots, peas, and celery. Cook an additional 10 minutes.

4. Add tomatoes, tomato sauce, corn, green beans, and more hot water if needed. Season with salt and pepper, put the lid on, and let simmer on medium until vegetables are tender.

5. Drop in cut okra and simmer for ten more minutes or until tender. Salt and pepper to taste and serve with hot cornbread.

Nan's Notes: *Adjust the amount of vegetables based on your taste—add a little more or a little less.*

Oyster Artichoke Soup

MAKES 4 SERVINGS

Tami Owen, Belinda Hicks Haeusler, and I were the three amigos in college at USM. When Tami learned about One Pan Nan, she called up and left the funniest message. She said, "I heard about One Pan Nan and wanted to know just what you're cooking in that one pan because you can't cook!" I laughed, and I think I could hear her laughing all the way from Texas to Tennessee! And she's right. I didn't know how to cook a bit back in college—all they knew was that I could eat.

Tami would make this soup all the time back then, and I called her up the other day to see if I could include it in the book. I think it surprised her that I remembered it, but this is something you can't easily forget. Good recipes and good friends always remain in the favorite parts of our memories.

1 stick butter
1 bunch green onions, chopped
½ cup chopped celery
1 cup chicken stock
1 (8-ounce) can quartered artichoke hearts, drained
1 quart fresh oysters, shucked, drained, and chopped
1 cup half-and-half
3 cups heavy cream
2 tablespoons Worcestershire sauce
Tabasco sauce

1. Melt butter in a large stockpot over medium heat. Sauté onions and celery until tender, about 10 minutes. Pour in chicken stock and reduce heat to low. Cook for about 10 minutes.

2. Add the artichokes and oysters and simmer for 10 minutes. Stir in the half-and-half and heavy cream. Add the Worcestershire sauce and pour in Tabasco to taste. Serve immediately.

Blue Cheese Tomato Soup

MAKES 4 SERVINGS

My favorite cold weather lunch that takes away the chill every time is tomato soup with a grilled cheese sandwich. You can't beat the classic condensed tomato soup, but this one sure gives it a hard run for its money.

It's a nice upgrade from the usual. It's hearty enough for your family and just fancy enough for company, too.

- 1 (28-ounce) can whole tomatoes in juice
- 1 tablespoon oil
- 1 medium onion, finely chopped
- 2 stalks celery, finely chopped
- 1 (14½-ounce) can chicken broth
- ¼ cup dry red wine
- 1½ teaspoons brown sugar
- 1 teaspoon dried thyme
- ½ cup half-and-half
- Blue cheese crumbles
- Salt and freshly ground black pepper

1. Pour tomatoes into a medium bowl and mash with a potato masher, crushing into small pieces.

2. In a saucepan, heat oil over medium-low heat. Add onions and celery, cover, and cook for 10 minutes. Stir in tomatoes, broth, wine, sugar, and thyme and heat to a boil. Reduce heat, cover, and simmer for 30 minutes or until vegetables are very tender.

3. Stir in cream and heat through. Ladle into bowls and sprinkle each with blue cheese crumbles. Season with salt and black pepper to taste and serve.

SALADS, SANDWICHES, SOUPS & STEWS 83

Southwest Taco Soup

MAKES 6 SERVINGS

PREPARATION TIME: 20 MINUTES • COOKING TIME: 40 MINUTES

Growing up in Hattiesburg, we rarely added a new dish to the repertoire because our taste buds were pretty set in their ways. However, somewhere along the way, taco soup became a regular at family meals down in Mississippi. Now it's a regular in Tennessee, too!

- 1 pound ground beef
- 1 large onion, chopped
- 5 or 6 celery stalks, chopped
- 1 package reduced-sodium taco seasoning
- 1 package ranch dressing mix
- 1 (14.5-ounce) can Red Gold® Diced Tomatoes
- 1 (10-ounce) can Red Gold® Petite Diced Tomatoes & Green Chilies
- 1 (14.5-ounce) can beef broth, lower sodium
- 1½ to 2 cups hot water
- 1 (15-ounce) can pinto beans with jalapeños (may add more, see note)
- 1 (8-ounce) can shoepeg corn

1. In a large stockpot, sauté ground beef, onions, and celery until beef has browned.

2. Add taco seasoning and ranch dressing mix and stir well. Add both cans of tomatoes, beef broth, and hot water and bring to a boil. Reduce heat and simmer for about 20 to 30 minutes.

3. Add beans and shoepeg corn right before serving and heat through. Serve with tortilla chips, grated cheese, and sour cream.

Nan's Notes: *If you'd like to add an extra can of pinto beans, also add an extra can of beef broth.*

Meatball Soup

MAKES 6 SERVINGS

They say you shouldn't go to the grocery store when you're hungry because you'll end up buying more than what is on your list. Then again, if you're like me, you might only go when you're hungry so you can hit all the sample stations! You might come away with a good recipe idea, like this one. Inspired by one of those empty-stomached grocery runs in search of a cure for my rumbling tummy.

1½ pounds ground beef

½ cup crushed saltine crackers

½ teaspoon Italian seasoning

1 egg, beaten

2 tablespoons pesto (recipe on page 35, or use store bought)

½ teaspoon salt, divided

¼ teaspoon black pepper

1 tablespoon vegetable oil

½ cup chopped onion

½ cup chopped celery

½ cup chopped green pepper

2 garlic cloves, minced

3 cups fresh spinach leaves

2 (15½-ounce) cans Great Northern beans, drained

1 (32-ounce) container chicken broth (I like the low salt)

Freshly grated Parmesan cheese

1. In a large bowl, combine ground beef, cracker crumbs, Italian seasoning, egg, pesto, ¼ teaspoon salt, and black pepper. Shape into 1-inch meatballs.

2. Heat oil in a large stockpot over medium-high and cook meatballs, on all sides, for about 8 minutes. Remove meatballs when done and set aside.

3. Add onion, celery, green pepper, and garlic to the pan and sauté until vegetables are tender. Add spinach and cook 2 to 3 minutes. Reduce heat to medium low.

4. Stir in beans, broth, meatballs, and remaining salt. Simmer 10 to 15 minutes or until meatballs and soup are hot. Top with cheese and serve.

Nan's Notes: *I like using saltine crackers for breadcrumbs because I always have saltines in the pantry, which is not always the case with breadcrumbs. For Italian breadcrumbs, just add a little Italian seasoning.*

BLT Soup

MAKES 4–6 SERVINGS

My friend Beth Farrer shared this delicious soup recipe with me. She and her husband Matt own a Gigi's Cupcakes in Florence, Kentucky. In addition to being a master cupcake baker, she's also a culinary school graduate, so her skills run the gamut when it comes to food.

Every year about the middle of December, Charlie starts watching the mail because he knows a box of his favorite cookies will soon arrive straight from Beth's kitchen. She's a wonderful woman with a giving heart—she and Matt are constantly supporting their community. If you ever pass through Florence, stop and have a Mississippi Mud cupcake for me, please.

- 3 tablespoons unsalted butter
- 1 medium onion, minced
- 1 medium carrot, minced
- 1 small stalk celery, minced
- 1 medium garlic clove, minced
- 4 to 6 strips bacon, cooked and crumbled
- 2 tablespoons flour
- 2½ cups low-sodium chicken stock
- 2½ cups half-and-half
- 1 bay leaf
- Pinch of cayenne pepper
- 6 ounces sharp Cheddar cheese, shredded (optional)
- Salt and freshly ground black pepper to taste
- 2 tomatoes, seeded and chopped
- 2 cups lettuce, cut into small shreds

1. Heat butter in large heavy-bottomed Dutch oven over medium heat until foaming. Add onion and cook, stirring occasionally, until softened, about 4 minutes. Add carrots, celery, garlic, and bacon. Cook until garlic is fragrant, about 1 minute. Add flour and cook, stirring to coat vegetables, until mixture begins to brown on bottom of pot, about 2 minutes.

2. Gradually whisk in chicken stock and half-and-half and add bay leaf. Increase heat to medium-high and bring to a boil. Reduce heat to medium-low and simmer until vegetables soften, about 10 minutes. Remove from heat and add cayenne pepper.

3. Cool soup 1 minute, slowly whisk in cheese, and season with salt and pepper. Ladle soup into individual bowls. Top each bowl with about ½ cup shredded lettuce and garnish with chopped tomato. Serve immediately.

My parents Bud and Gloria Sumrall on a trip to Nashville. This was the weekend that Momma let me cook for her!

Momma

I am blessed and fortunate to have traveled to many places around the world and enjoyed some wonderful meals. The Brussels sprouts at the Red Lion in Hockwold, England have never been beaten. The fresh, handmade pasta from a generous host family in Sardinia, Italy was amazing, and the creamiest crème brûlée I have ever had was at a French restaurant, believe it or not, in Mexico City, Mexico. And growing up in south Mississippi has left me with memories of the finest examples of southern fare. At the end of the day, however, it is my momma's cooking that is the most comforting and closest to my heart.

My mother, Gloria Jean, has cooked all her life, having learned from her mother, Elsie Broome. Nannie Broome as I called her, was a school teacher and when Momma was little, she would ride home from school with Nannie and get supper going while Nannie graded papers. Then when Paw Paw Lonnie got home from a long day of pipefitting, they would all sit down and eat. So my mother grew up in front of the stove and knows how to do it and do it well…in my humble opinion of course!

My brother Denny, my sister Kim, and I each have our favorite meals that Momma makes for us. For me, it's her chicken and dumplings, red beans & rice, and turnip greens and cornbread. Somehow between working full time and taking care of us three as kids, she managed to cook these dishes that are permanently imprinted in my mind and on my palate. When she cooks, she puts everything she's got into it—from going through the greens microscopically to pick out the bad ones to monitoring the dumplings, making sure they don't stick and tasting them constantly in order to get the ratio of broth to cream just right. She nurses each meal and pampers the process.

These days, whenever I make a trip back to Hattiesburg, one of my favorite meals is always on the stove waiting for me. Before my bags hit the floor, I head for the stove to see what's cooking. Momma hears me before she sees me. That unmistakable sound of the fork clanging against the sides of the pot tells her I have arrived. "Natalie Jo! I hear you," she calls out from somewhere in the house. She feigns frustration because I'm not using a plate and sitting at the table in a more dignified manner, but I can hear the secret satisfaction in her voice. Once we finally do sit down for that proper meal, she knows with every trip I make back to the stove that she has made me happy and that makes her happy. That is a lot of happy because I make several trips.

No matter how many times I try to make these dishes myself, they never taste the same; there really is something in a mother's touch. It is that extra love they put into everything they do for their children—from washing clothes to drying tears, and in my case, from perming hair to preparing meals. Mothers always do things a little better than anyone else. My momma has shown me love in many ways, but I feel it most when I am sitting in front of a plate full of her cooking. So, I say yes to the words of William Ross Wallace, "For the hand that rocks the cradle is the hand that rules the world." And my belly!

Not-So-Typical Broccoli Cheese Soup

MAKES 6–8 SERVINGS

Some people may not have a whole lotta love for broccoli, but my husband does. I think we have it at the house at least a couple of times a week. It's good that Charlie likes it though because it's at the top of the "good for you" list of veggies. One winter, we were trapped at home here in Nashville for several days because of bad ice and freezing temperatures and when our driveway freezes, there's no getting down it unless you're skating, skiing, or sledding. Luckily, I had a big pot of this going in the slow cooker when the freeze set in, so we ate it for several days in a row. We may have been stuck, but we sure weren't starving!

- 2 tablespoons butter
- 1 medium onion, chopped
- 1½ teaspoons minced garlic
- 1 cup shredded carrots
- 6 tablespoons flour
- Salt and freshly ground black pepper
- 1 (12-ounce) and 1 (5-ounce) cans evaporated milk
- 4½ cups low-sodium chicken broth
- 4 cups fresh broccoli florets, trimmed down to be equally-sized
- ⅛ teaspoon dried thyme
- ½ teaspoon crushed red pepper flakes
- ⅛ teaspoon nutmeg
- ½ cup half-and-half (may add more)
- 2 cups freshly shredded Cheddar cheese

1. Melt butter in a slow cooker pan over medium heat on the stovetop (make sure your pan is stovetop safe). Add onions and sauté until they begin to soften, about 3 to 4 minutes. Add garlic and flour and season lightly with salt and pepper. Cook for 2 minutes, stirring constantly. Slowly pour in both cans of evaporated milk and whisk well to smooth. Cook mixture, stirring constantly until it begins to thicken and then move pan over to slow cooker base.

2. Add in chicken broth, broccoli, thyme, red pepper flakes, and nutmeg. Cover and cook on high for 2½ to 3 hours or on low for 6 hours. Turn setting to warm (or off) and stir in half-and-half and shredded Cheddar cheese. Season to taste with salt and pepper and serve.

Nan's Notes: *There are plenty of recipes out there for broccoli cheese soup. It's like chili or potato cheese soup—it's a personal taste. I use fresh broccoli instead of frozen, I add some carrots, and I like adding the red pepper flakes early on in the process to put in a little heat. Add more if you like a spicier flavor.*

Potato & Bacon Chowder

MAKES 6 SERVINGS

This is one of those "Christmas Eve-worthy" soups. I made it one year just for variety. I love the shredded carrots and white wine…and the bacon… and the half-and-half. Heck, what's not to love about this!

6 slices bacon
2 cups kernel corn, drained
1 onion, chopped
1 (15-ounce) can chicken broth
1 cup water
2 large russet potatoes, peeled and cubed
1½ teaspoons dried thyme
2 teaspoons dried parsley
¼ cup shredded carrots
½ cup dry white wine
1 cup half-and-half
1 tablespoon butter
Freshly ground black pepper

1. In a large stockpot, cook bacon until crispy. Set aside. Drain bacon grease from pot, leaving a tablespoon or two for sautéing.

2. Add corn and onion to stockpot and sauté on medium low until onions are tender. Add chicken broth, water, potatoes, thyme, parsley, and carrots. Increase heat to medium-high and boil while stirring occasionally. Remove pan from heat and pour in the wine.

3. Bring to a boil again and reduce heat to simmer. Cook until potatoes are tender. Using a hand blender, pulse to blend, but do not puree until smooth.

4. Pour in half-and-half and add butter. Stir until blended well. Add bacon and black pepper to taste and serve.

Nan's Notes: *If you're using fresh herbs instead of dried, increase the amount by 2 or 3 times.*

Bean Chowder

MAKES 6 SERVINGS

This recipe goes in the "must serve with cornbread" category. Bacon, beans, and cornbread...that's Being Southern 101. You could also go with KK's Corn Dodgers (recipe on page 97) for a bit of a Yankee spin.

- 1½ cups dried navy beans, rinsed
- 6 slices bacon
- 1 large carrot, cut into 1-inch sticks, plus ¼ cup shredded carrots for garnish
- 1 celery stalk, chopped
- 1½ cups chopped onion
- 1 small turnip, cut into 1-inch pieces
- 1 tablespoon dried thyme
- ⅛ teaspoon black pepper
- 1 (48-ounce) container reduced-sodium chicken broth
- 1 cup milk
- Dash of Tabasco sauce

1. Soak beans overnight in a bowl of cold water. Drain and set aside.

2. Cook bacon in slow cooker pan on stovetop (ensure pan is safe for stovetop). Remove bacon when done, crumble, and set aside, reserving 2 tablespoons for garnish.

3. Drain drippings from the pan. Transfer pan to base of slow cooker, and add carrot sticks, celery, onion, turnip, thyme, black pepper, beans, and bacon. Pour in chicken broth and mix. Cover and cook on low for 7½ to 9 hours or until beans are tender.

4. Using an immersion stick hand blender, pulse for a few seconds in 2 areas of the pan. Add milk and Tabasco, and gently stir to blend. Heat for an additional 10 minutes or more. Garnish with reserved bacon crumbles and shredded carrots for serving.

SALADS, SANDWICHES, SOUPS & STEWS

Turkey & Sausage Gumbo

MAKES 6 SERVINGS

PREPARATION TIME: 20 MINUTES • COOKING TIME: 45 MINUTES

- 2 tablespoons bacon grease
- 2 heaping tablespoons flour
- 1 pound frozen chopped okra (can also use fresh)
- 2 large onions, diced
- 1 large green pepper, diced
- 1 (14.5-ounce) can Red Gold® Diced Tomatoes
- 1 quart chicken stock
- 2 bay leaves
- 3 quarts hot water
- 1 pound turkey meat, cooked and cut into small chunks
- 1 pound Andouille sausage, cooked and cut into slices
- ½ teaspoon Creole seasoning (may add more to taste)
- 2 teaspoons gumbo filé powder (found in the seafood dept. at my grocery store)
- Zatarain's liquid crab boil, to taste (optional)
- Hot, cooked white rice

1. In a large stockpot, heat bacon grease. Add flour and stir constantly to make the roux. Brown until the flour's color is very dark. Add okra, onions, and peppers and cook until okra is stringy, stirring frequently.

2. Add tomatoes, chicken stock, bay leaves, and hot water. Heat this mixture to a boil and then reduce heat. Add turkey, Andouille sausage, and Creole seasoning and simmer for at least 30 minutes or until vegetables are tender. May simmer longer.

3. While hot, add gumbo filé powder and stir. Gumbo can be kept hot on a low temp, but do not boil again once file has been added. If desired, add a dash of the liquid crab boil to the entire pot, to taste. Remove bay leaves before serving over rice.

Nan's Notes: *The secret to good gumbo is the roux. Make sure to get the roux nice and brown. Stir the flour/bacon grease mixture constantly so it doesn't burn. This takes a few minutes. Be patient, keep stirring, and cook until it is deep brown. Make this up the day before you want to serve or at least early on the day of, as the flavors come together and meld with a little time. The liquid crab boil is good, but it's really hot, so use it sparingly if you add it to the pot. You can always make it spicier, but you can't undo the heat once it's in there. Trust me on this one—I've made Charlie's face sweat many times by going too heavy with the crab boil! Serve with plenty of crusty French bread toasted with butter, garlic powder, and a pinch of salt.*

In my thoroughly scrubbed and propped-out-for-television kitchen.

No Leftover Leftovers

The *Top 20 Countdown* crew from Great American Country came out to the house one fall to shoot a Thanksgiving week episode. Producer Dottie wanted to offer the viewers a recipe option for the leftover turkey, and this was my contribution to the thousands already out there. Basically, I took my Seafood Gumbo recipe and replaced the shrimp and crabmeat with turkey and Andouille sausage. We had a big crew working on the show, and when we were done shooting, we just about ate the whole pot of gumbo!

All of us stood in the kitchen and gobbled it up (pun intended). TV folks are hard workers, and food is important. I've had hundreds of fun crew meals with my camera, audio, and tech friends over the years, but it was especially satisfying to get to cook for them. I hope they tasted my appreciation in every bite!

SALADS, SANDWICHES, SOUPS & STEWS

KK's Chili

MAKES 6 SERVINGS

Only the grandkids call Miss Pat "KK," but the whole family calls this chili their favorite. Charlie won't eat this without the corn dodgers, and they're tricky to get right. You can make them crunchy all the way through, or they can have a slightly soft center. Either way, when you smear them with butter and dip them into your chili, it's a match made in culinary heaven.

1 to 1½ pounds ground beef

1 medium onion, chopped

1 teaspoon chili powder

3 (10¾-ounce) cans condensed tomato soup

3 (15½-ounce) cans dark kidney beans

Shredded Cheddar cheese (optional)

CORN DODGERS:

1 cup cornmeal

1 teaspoon salt

1½ teaspoons sugar

2 tablespoons melted butter

1. Brown ground beef in a deep skillet. Add the onion and cook until tender. Add tomato soup and beans. Cook about 15 minutes.

2. Add chili powder and simmer on low for at least 20 minutes, stirring occasionally. May simmer longer. Serve with shredded Cheddar cheese on top.

3. *For Corn Dodgers:* In a medium bowl, mix all ingredients together. Pour 1¼ cups boiling water over the mixture and stir to blend. Drop by the spoonful onto a greased baking sheet. Use a fork to flatten out so they are thin. Bake at 400° F for about 20 minutes, depending on how thick they are. You can also flip them over after the initial 20 minutes just to make sure they are crisp on both sides. You want them to be good and crunchy on the edges. Serve hot with lots of butter.

Nan's Notes: *Chili is good to keep in the freezer for those winter days when it gets dark way too early, and you don't have a plan for dinner. This is on the mild side, so add more chili powder if you like it hot. For the dodgers, don't make the mistake of using cornmeal mix instead of cornmeal. Doesn't work. Lesson learned.*

Green Chile Chili

MAKES 6–8 SERVINGS

There are plenty of great-tasting white chicken chili recipes floating around, but this is really more about the green than the white. This recipe came about because of necessity. Spring was supposed to be heading our way one March, and lo and behold, the temperature here in Nashville dropped to 29 degrees! I headed to the kitchen for some hot comfort food in the form of lots of green chilies. Verde enchilada sauce is made from green chilies and with the two additional cans of diced green chilies, it's definitely all about the green!

- 1 tablespoon olive oil
- 1 large onion, chopped
- 3 garlic cloves, minced
- 2 large chicken breasts, cut into chunks
- 2½ teaspoons cumin
- ¼ teaspoon dried oregano
- ½ teaspoon hot Mexican chili powder
- 2 teaspoons dried cilantro
- 1 (32-ounce) container low sodium chicken broth
- 1 (10-ounce) can verde enchilada sauce
- 2 (4-ounce) cans diced green chilies
- 3 (15½-ounce) cans great northern beans, drained
- Tortilla strips
- Monterey Jack cheese
- Sour cream
- Chopped fresh cilantro

1. Using the pan of the slow cooker on the stovetop (ensure that your pan is stovetop safe), sauté onion and garlic in olive oil over medium-high heat for 3 or 4 minutes. Add in the chicken and sauté until brown, but not done.

2. Remove pan from stovetop and transfer to base of slow cooker. Sprinkle in the cumin, oregano, chili powder, and cilantro and stir to evenly coat. Pour in chicken broth, enchilada sauce, and green chilies and stir to blend. Cook on high heat for one hour.

3. Pour in two cans of the beans. Empty third can onto a plate and smash beans with a fork. Add plate of beans to the slow cooker. Stir to blend and cook on high for an additional one hour or until chicken is done and chili has thickened. Serve with cornbread or tortilla chips, Monterey jack cheese, and sour cream. Garnish with cilantro.

Vegetarian Chili

MAKES 6 SERVINGS

My sweet Daddy is pretty much a meat-and-three kind of guy. Or if it's a casserole or stew, he really wants and appreciates the protein factor, but I think even he wouldn't miss the meat at all in this. This is from my sister-in-law Anne Kelley's kitchen, and she and I agree that this colorful, flavorful dish gets even better the second day when all the spices meld together.

- 1 tablespoon olive oil
- 2 cups chopped onion
- ½ cup chopped yellow pepper
- ½ cup chopped green pepper
- 2 garlic cloves, minced
- 1 tablespoon brown sugar
- 2 tablespoons chili powder
- 1½ teaspoons cumin
- 1½ teaspoons oregano
- 1 teaspoon salt
- ½ teaspoon black pepper
- 2 (16-ounce) cans stewed tomatoes, undrained
- 2 (15½-ounce) cans black beans, rinsed and drained
- 1 (15½-ounce) can kidney beans, rinsed and drained
- 1 (15½-ounce) can pinto beans, rinsed and drained
- Shredded Cheddar cheese
- Sour cream

1. Heat oil in large stockpot. Add onion, yellow peppers, green peppers, and garlic and sauté until vegetables are tender.
2. Add brown sugar, chili powder, cumin, oregano, salt, and pepper. Stir well. Add tomatoes and all beans and blend to mix. Simmer for at least 30 minutes. Serve with shredded Cheddar and sour cream.

Southwestern Sirloin Stew

MAKES 6 SERVINGS

My parents came up from Mississippi one weekend, and we weren't sure what time they were going to get here or how hungry they were going to be. But I wanted to have something good ready for them just in case, and this hit the mark. We all had seconds, and Momma loved it! It made me happy to make her happy, and Daddy was happy because we had Blue Bell ice cream for dessert!

- 2 pounds sirloin steak, cut into chunks
- 1 (28-ounce) can whole tomatoes, undrained
- 1 (14 ½-ounce) can beef broth (low sodium version)
- 1 large onion, chopped
- 1½ teaspoons Mexican chili powder
- 1 teaspoon cumin
- 1 (1¼-ounce) envelope taco seasoning
- 1 (15-ounce) can black beans, rinsed and drained
- 1 (11-ounce) can whole kernel corn with red and green peppers, drained
- Shredded Cheddar or Mexican flavored cheese
- Sour cream
- Fresh chopped cilantro

1. Mix beef, tomatoes, broth, onions, chili powder, and cumin in slow cooker. Cover and cook on low for 9 to 11 hours or until beef is tender.

2. Stir in taco seasoning and mix. Add in beans and corn and stir to blend. Cover and cook for about ½ hour to allow sauce to thicken. Serve with cheese and sour cream. Garnish with cilantro, if desired.

Fennel Chicken Stew

MAKES 8 SERVINGS

I attended a women's retreat a few years ago with a beautiful group of ladies. It was an uplifting weekend with some delicious food prepared by Jane McCracken—like this stew. Jane shared her recipe with me, and I made it for Christmas Eve that year instead of doing seafood gumbo. The food you serve on Christmas Eve should be as special as the evening itself and this certainly was.

- 2 medium leeks
- 1 fennel bulb (about 1 pound)
- 2 tablespoons olive oil
- 2 tablespoons butter
- 1 pound skinless boneless chicken, chopped
- 8 ounces mushrooms, quartered
- 4 medium carrots, chopped into small pieces
- 1 pound small red potatoes, quartered
- 2 bay leaves
- ¼ teaspoon dried tarragon leaves
- 1 teaspoon dried thyme
- 1 (15-ounce) can chicken broth
- ½ cup dry white wine
- 1¼ cups half-and-half
- 3 tablespoons flour
- ¾ teaspoon salt
- 1 cup frozen peas
- Salt and freshly ground black pepper

1. Cut off roots of leeks and trim leafy ends. Cut each leek in half lengthwise and then cut crosswise into ¾-inch pieces. Place in a large bowl of cold water and move them around thoroughly with your hands, separating pieces to remove dirt. Scoop leeks out of the water and set aside on a towel to drain.

2. Cut root end and stalks from fennel bulb and discard. Cut bulb lengthwise into thin wedges. In a large stockpot, heat olive oil over medium heat. Add butter and melt. Add chicken and cook until chicken is golden brown and just loses its pink color throughout. Remove chicken and set aside on a plate. Add mushrooms to same pot and cook until golden. Remove and set aside with chicken. Add more olive oil and butter. Put in leeks, fennel, carrots, potatoes, bay leaves, tarragon, thyme, chicken broth, and wine. Cook until tender (about 20 minutes).

3. In a small bowl, mix half-and-half with flour until smooth. Stir into vegetable mixture. Add chicken, mushrooms, and peas. Season with salt and pepper to taste and cook for another 10 minutes. Remove bay leaves before serving. Serve with crusty bread.

Nan's Notes: *Be sure to rinse off all the dirt on the leek while trimming. Gritty stew is not good!*

Lunch & Dinner

Margherita Pizza

MAKES 8 SERVINGS

I love margherita pizza. I always choose it when I walk up to a by-the-slice pizza counter. A traditional one consists of 3 ingredients only—tomatoes, mozzarella, and fresh basil, and according to legend, it's named after one of Italy's queens and represents the colors of the Italian flag. While I love the traditional version, I wanted to spice it up a bit with some red pepper flakes, roasted garlic, and chicken. So, I hope Queen Margherita would not have objected to me taking a few liberties with her namesake…at least I kept to the color scheme.

Olive oil for sautéing

2 garlic cloves, ends removed but skin on

Salt and freshly ground black pepper

1 chicken breast

1 (12- to 14-ounce) can refrigerated pizza dough

1 (15-ounce) can tomato sauce

1 teaspoon red pepper flakes (may use more or less to taste)

8 ounces fresh mozzarella cheese, chopped

¼ cup coarsely chopped fresh basil

1. In a medium skillet, add about a teaspoon of olive oil and sauté whole garlic cloves on each side until lightly browned. Remove and cool.

2. To same skillet, add additional olive oil and allow to heat up. Season each side of chicken breast with salt and pepper and pan fry until done. Set aside to cool.

3. Preheat oven to appropriate temperature per dough's directions. Roll out dough onto a baking sheet. Pour ⅔ can tomato sauce onto dough and spread evenly to about ½ inch from the edge. Refrigerate remaining sauce.

4. Chop cooked chicken breast into bite-sized pieces. Remove skin from cooled garlic cloves, mince, and sprinkle evenly onto sauce. Top with red pepper flakes, mozzarella cheese, chopped basil, and chicken.

5. Bake according to instructions on dough package and serve hot.

BLT Pizza

MAKES 8 SERVINGS

After a One Pan Nan shoot at the house one day, we wanted to feed the camera crew—that is always important! Charlie went to Jet's Pizza and grabbed a couple of pies to go. He came back with a standard pepperoni and took a chance on another called a BLT. I've been a long-time fan of the sandwich, but I wasn't so sure about a pizza. What a delicious surprise and a lighter-tasting alternative. Here is my version.

- 1 (12-inch) prepared pizza crust
- ½ cup mayonnaise
- 1 teaspoon dried basil (if using fresh, double or triple the amount)
- ½ teaspoon garlic powder
- ¼ teaspoon onion powder
- Salt and freshly ground black pepper
- ¾ cup grated Cheddar cheese
- ¾ cup grated Mozzarella cheese
- 5 to 7 ounces bacon bits (reserve 1 tablespoon for topping)
- 1½ to 2 cups shredded iceberg lettuce
- 2 medium tomatoes, sliced

1. Preheat oven according to crust's directions. Mix mayonnaise, basil, garlic powder, and onion powder in a small bowl. Season with salt and pepper. Spread mayonnaise mixture onto pizza dough.

2. Cover with both cheeses and bacon bits. Bake pizza according to crust's directions.

3. When done, remove from oven and evenly sprinkle lettuce on top. Place tomatoes slices on lettuce and top with reserved bacon bits. Serve immediately.

Grilled Cheese & Herb Pizza

MAKES 8 SERVINGS

Why haven't I been cooking pizza on the grill my whole adult life?? I was out shopping one day and saw a pizza grilling stone and humongous pizza paddle set, and I had to get it. That night, I grilled this pizza, and I haven't looked back at the oven since. Now in the dead of winter, I might snuggle back up to my oven, but when summertime rolls around, the grill is my guy. If you've never cooked with a pizza stone, prepare yourself for the crispiest crust ever.

1 (12-inch) prepared pizza crust

2 large tomatoes, sliced

Olive oil

1 (4-ounce) container feta cheese

½ cup chopped fresh basil

2 garlic cloves, roasted and minced

1 teaspoon salt

½ teaspoon freshly ground black pepper

1 teaspoon red pepper flakes

Spoonful of cornmeal

1. Place pizza stone on lower rack of grill and turn grill burners to low, allowing stone and grill to preheat for about 10 minutes. While grill and stone preheat, spread sliced tomatoes on a plate and drizzle with olive oil. In a small bowl, combine feta cheese, basil, garlic, salt, and black pepper and stir.

2. Lay pizza crust on a pizza paddle (or a baking sheet with no sides) and top with tomatoes. Spoon cheese and basil mixture evenly on top of tomatoes and sprinkle with red pepper flakes.

3. Dust a little cornmeal on the hot pizza stone to prevent sticking and carefully slide pizza onto stone. Close the grill lid and cook for approximately 7 to 10 minutes, depending on the temperature of your grill.

4. Pizza is ready when crust is golden brown. Use pizza paddle to remove pizza. Slice and serve. Allow stone to cool completely before removing from grill.

Nan's Notes: *The cooking time may take a little longer if you have a charcoal grill.*

Spinach & Feta Bake

MAKES 6 SERVINGS

I really hated cutting into this dish when it came out of the oven. It was so pretty, but I got over that real quick and dove in. It tastes just as good as it looks. That's not always the case—pretty food doesn't always taste good. Take my word for it, this one's got looks, style...and taste!

1 tablespoon olive oil

5 green onions, chopped (include white bulb and ½ way up green stem)

1 (16-ounce) bag frozen chopped spinach, thawed and squeezed dry

4 tablespoons butter, melted

2 eggs

1 (15-ounce) container ricotta cheese

1 (4-ounce) package crumbled feta cheese

2 tablespoons dried oregano

1½ teaspoons garlic salt

¼ teaspoon black pepper

⅛ teaspoon ground nutmeg

1 (8-ounce) roll frozen phyllo pastry sheets, thawed in original package (approximately 9 x 14 inches each)

1. In a medium skillet, heat oil and sauté green onions on medium heat for 3 or 4 minutes.

2. Add in spinach, stir to blend, and cook for an additional 4 minutes. Remove from burner to cool.

3. Preheat oven to 350° F. Brush a 9 x 13-inch baking dish lightly with melted butter. Beat eggs in medium bowl. Stir in spinach and onion mixture, ricotta cheese, feta cheese, oregano, garlic salt, pepper, and nutmeg. Set aside.

4. Open package of thawed pastry sheets and unroll. Keep dough covered per package directions while assembling pie. Place one piece of dough in dish and brush top lightly with melted butter. Repeat for the next 6 sheets of dough.

5. Spoon spinach mixture evenly over dough. Top spinach mixture with sheet of dough and brush lightly with butter. Repeat this process for the next 6 sheets of dough. Bake uncovered for 35 to 40 minutes or until golden brown.

Nan's Notes: *Working with phyllo pastry dough is very easy; just don't be in a hurry. And if you tear a sheet, don't worry about it—just lay it in and line up the seams. There are many layers, and the butter helps to meld it all together. This dish is a perfect meatless lunch or light dinner option. Add some fruit or a salad and you are good to go. It tastes great cold from the fridge the next day, too—I grab a piece for the road and eat it like a sandwich.*

Eggplant Casserole

MAKES 6 SERVINGS

This is my great grandmother's recipe. It was in my nannie's handwritten recipe book with the title "Mama's Eggplant Casserole." I remember eating this many times at Nannie's house. I don't think Grannie Watts would mind that I added oregano and paprika, do you?

- 4 tablespoons oil or bacon drippings
- ½ cup chopped onion
- ½ cup chopped green pepper
- 1 pound ground beef
- 1 large eggplant, peeled and chopped into crouton-sized pieces
- 1 (14½-ounce) can diced tomatoes
- 3 tablespoons dried oregano
- 1 teaspoon smoked sweet paprika
- 2 tablespoons sugar
- Salt and freshly ground black pepper to taste
- 1 cup grated sharp Cheddar cheese
- 1 cup breadcrumbs

1. Heat oil in a large skillet or flameproof casserole on medium-high. Sauté onions, green peppers, ground beef, and eggplant for 10 minutes.

2. Add tomatoes, oregano, paprika, sugar, and salt and pepper to taste. Cover and cook for 10 minutes, stirring occasionally.

3. If using a skillet, pour into a greased 2-quart baking dish or continue with flameproof casserole. Cover with cheese and breadcrumbs and bake at 400° F for 20 minutes.

Pasta Con Verdure Fresche
(Pasta with Fresh Vegetables)

MAKES 6–8 SERVINGS

(From our video recipe shoot with singer/songwriter Victoria Venier)

- 4 tablespoons olive oil
- 3 garlic cloves, finely minced
- 1 small sweet onion, finely chopped
- 2 cups chopped mushrooms
- ½ red bell pepper, chopped
- ½ yellow bell pepper, chopped
- 1 small zucchini, chopped
- 1 yellow squash, chopped (optional)
- ½ cup chopped fresh parsley
- 1 cup fresh spinach
- 1 tablespoon Nature's Seasoning spice mix
- 6 (15-ounce) cans organic tomato sauce or homemade sauce of same amount
- 2 tablespoons chopped fresh basil
- 2 tablespoons chopped fresh oregano
- 1 teaspoon chopped fresh thyme
- 1 tablespoon crushed red pepper
- 1 tablespoon sugar
- Sea salt to taste
- 1 cup freshly grated Asiago and Parmesan cheese
- 1 box short cut pasta (your choice)

1. Heat a large Dutch oven on medium-high heat. Pour in olive oil and sauté garlic, onions, and mushrooms until tender.

2. Add in peppers and zucchini and continue sautéing until tender. Add in the parsley, spinach, and a little bit of the Nature's Seasoning and stir to blend.

3. Once the vegetables are tender but not overcooked, add the tomato sauce. Sprinkle in basil, oregano, thyme, and the remainder of the Nature's Seasoning and blend.

4. Add crushed red pepper and sugar. Stir together and bring to a light boil. Reduce heat to low and cover. Simmer for at least one hour.

5. Boil pasta to al dente and drain. Add pasta to sauce, salt to taste, and stir well. Serve with generous portions of grated cheese on the top.

Victoria and I with her delizioso pasta and homemade bread!

Tasty Tunes & Perfect Pasta

This recipe for **Pasta Con Verdure Fresche** is from a talented friend of mine, Victoria Venier. She and her husband Matt own a production company just north of Nashville in White House, Tennessee, and if you've seen a show at a theme park lately, chances are it was a Matt Davenport Production. Victoria is VP of the company and does the vocal coaching for their performers, but the heart of this talented gal lives for songwriting, and she knows her way around a lyric and a melody. In fact, her song "Back To You" landed on the Grammy-nominated Take 6 record *The Standard*.

When she's not coaching or writing songs, she's touring the country with her trio, Hits & Grins. As if all that wasn't enough, she can cook, too. Where she finds the time I don't know, but her Italian roots shine through in the kitchen, and this dish is proof. Her greatest gift though is that she is an encouraging friend with a heart of gold.

Me, Victoria, and Matt—"Papa Con Verdure & The Fresche Girls" working on a One Pan Nan jingle.

LUNCH & DINNER

Hoppin' John

MAKES 6–8 SERVINGS

According to Southern tradition, you should eat black-eyed peas on New Year's Day to bring good luck and prosperity in the New Year. Me? I could eat black-eyed peas every day of the year, and this dish is appropriate for anytime.

This has some jambalaya influence from my friend Robert St. John, using Andouille Sausage instead of bacon or a ham hock and some chicken and rice influence from momma, cooking the rice in the pot with the peas instead of just serving them over rice. It's a winner at the house. Charlie had two helpings of this the first time I made it. He is my Punxsutawney Phil of recipe taste testing. I wait with bated breath to see if I have a winner, or if I've got six more weeks in the kitchen to perfect a dish.

- 1 package (14½-ounce) Andouille sausage (or Cajun-style sausage), cut in half length wise and sliced in quarters
- 1 onion, chopped
- 2 stalks celery, chopped
- 1 heaping teaspoon minced garlic (may add more to taste)
- 3 cups low-sodium chicken broth
- 1 pound frozen black-eyed peas
- 1½ cups uncooked long grain rice (I used basmati)
- 1 large bay leaf or 2 small ones
- Salt and freshly ground black pepper

1. Preheat a large cast iron Dutch oven on medium-high heat on the stovetop. Add sausage and decrease heat to medium.

2. Add celery, onions, and garlic and cook together for about 8 to 10 minutes, stirring often.

3. Add chicken broth, black-eyed peas, rice, and bay leaf. Stir to blend. Cover and increase heat to medium-high. Bring to a bubbling simmer and stir.

4. Decrease heat to low, cover, and cook for about 20 to 30 minutes.

5. Remove from the heat and let rest with the lid on for about 5 minutes. Serve with garlic bread.

Gloria's Red Beans & Rice

MAKES 6–8 SERVINGS

My momma's red beans & rice recipe. No telling how many times I've enjoyed this dish. Hope you enjoy it too!

- 1 pound Camellia brand red beans (or your favorite brand)
- 1 or 2 bacon slices
- 1 onion, chopped
- 3 garlic cloves, crushed
- Salt and freshly ground black pepper
- 2 or 3 bay leaves
- 1 (8-ounce) can tomato sauce
- 1 pound package Cajun smoked sausage, sliced (Momma likes Polk's brand)
- Hot, cooked white rice

1. Soak beans overnight in water or soak at least 3 to 4 hours prior to cooking. Wash and pick out any debris.

2. Place the beans in a large stockpot. Add enough water to cover completely, plus several additional inches. Add bacon, onion, and garlic. Season with salt and pepper and drop in bay leaves. Cook on medium heat for 1 to 2 hours or until tender. Add water as needed and stir occasionally to prevent sticking.

3. While beans are cooking, brown sausage in a large skillet and drain on paper towels when done. Set aside.

4. When beans are tender, pour in tomato sauce, turn heat to medium, and continue to simmer for 30 more minutes. Add sausage to beans and stir to combine.

5. Mash a few of the cooked beans with a fork on the side of the pan and stir to blend. Cook on low for 10 to 15 minutes more, allowing beans to thicken. Serve over hot white rice with buttered, garlic French bread.

LUNCH & DINNER

Vacation

Food was so much a part of our family growing up that the social gatherings were mapped out around the food. We would be sitting around talking about this casserole and that cobbler, when somebody would say, "Hey, that would be good to have at a family reunion." The next thing you know, the whole clan was meeting up at the community center. Aunts, uncles, and first, second, and third cousins twice removed—all with their assigned covered dishes in hand. Even our family vacations were planned around food. On one such trip, we loaded up in the Buick and headed down to Pensacola, Florida. Momma and Daddy driving the car up front and us three kids driving them crazy in the back.

Now, most people pick a hotel based on amenities, price, or proximity to the beach, if that's where you're headed. But not my family! We picked the hotel that was closest to Shipley's Donuts. We may have had a twenty-minute drive to the beach, but we were driving there happy with our sack full of donut holes and those little orange juice bottles with the peel-back, foil lids.

On some vacations, the destination would be so foreign to Momma that her concern for our meals would overwhelm the reality of just how much space was available in the car. One Christmas, we decided to go snow skiing and the whole family drove—yes I said drove—from Hattiesburg, Mississippi, all the way out to Breckenridge, Colorado, in a Ford Bronco II. The Bronco II was kind of like the Chevette of SUVs, if that helps paint the picture of just how much interior space we were working with. Momma, fearing that the wild west of Colorado might not have anything edible at all, made up several batches of red beans & rice and spaghetti sauce, froze them, put them in an ice chest, and stuck it in the car before the suitcases. We might be wearing the same clothes for the week in Breckenridge, but we were not going hungry! That ice chest was always priority number one, along with paper towels, peanuts, and Pringles because wherever we were headed, those might be in short supply, too.

With my brother Denny and my sister Kim

That Christmas day in Colorado, we skied, we sang some Christmas carols, and laughed as Momma tried to make her way down the bunny slope. She's a much better cook than a skier. And that night, there may not have been any chestnuts roasting on an open fire, but there sure was a big pot of red beans & rice simmering on the stove.

Creamy Cajun Corn & Shrimp with Bacon

MAKES 4 SERVINGS

Some of the best food in the world is down in Louisiana, and I was fortunate to grow up just 100 miles or so from New Orleans. My momma probably wouldn't agree with that statement given the nights that she waited up until we got home safely from the French Quarter, but that's another story!

Louisiana has its own culture, and the food birthed out of that culture is unique and delicious. With relatives there and being so close to Hattiesburg, Cajun and Creole food make for a large percentage of our regular dishes. This one-pan recipe is full of fresh ingredients, big on flavor, and it's quick and easy, so you can enjoy a little bit of the Big Easy wherever you are. Laissez les bon temps rouler!

- 1 pound shrimp, peeled and deveined
- Salt and freshly ground black pepper
- 1 to 2 tablespoons butter
- 6 slices bacon, coarsely chopped
- 2 Roma tomatoes, seeded and diced
- ½ cup diced onions
- ½ cup diced green pepper
- 3 ears fresh corn, husks and silks removed
- 1 tablespoon blackening seasoning
- ½ cup half-and-half
- 1 tablespoon chives, chopped (for garnish)

1. Season the shrimp with salt and pepper and sauté in butter in a large skillet over medium-high heat. Shrimp will turn pink in color when done, about 2 to 3 minutes. Remove from pan and cover to keep warm.

2. Add bacon to the same pan and cook 3 to 4 minutes or until crisp. Drain the bacon drippings, reserving one tablespoon in pan. Stir in tomatoes, onions, and green pepper and cook for 2 to 3 minutes or until soft.

3. Slice corn from the cobs, scraping the cobs with the back of the knife to release remaining juices. Place corn in a mixing bowl and add blackening seasoning and half-and-half. Stir to mix. Pour corn mixture into pan and reduce heat to medium-low. Cook for 3 to 4 minutes, stirring frequently.

4. Add the shrimp to the pan and stir to combine. Cook until heated through. Serve immediately, topping each serving with chives, if desired.

Emmy Award-winning meteorologist Lelan Statom from NewsChannel 5 and I had some TV fun cookin' up this dish on "Talk of the Town."

Nan's Notes: *You can add fish to this instead of shrimp or for an authentic Cajun experience, add some crawfish. Serve it with a crusty French bread, topped with garlic butter.*

LUNCH & DINNER   117

Sweet & Sour Halibut

MAKES 6 SERVINGS

Our good friends Nick and Amy Ausman own the Crystal Bay Lodge in Petersburg, Alaska (shown at left). The beauty of that place is equaled only by the kindness of its owners. Amy runs the lodge and cooks all the meals with attention to every detail (this one is a favorite of her guests), while her son Captain Tyler takes guests out for some incredible fishing, whale watching, or glacier and sight seeing tours. Adventure in the most incredible surroundings with great accommodations and outstanding food…that's my kind of vacation.

1½ to 2 pounds halibut, cut into 1-inch cubes

Salt and freshly ground black pepper

Flour

Butter and oil for sautéing

1 (20-ounce) can pineapple chunks, drained and syrup reserved

½ cup brown sugar

2 tablespoons cornstarch

⅓ cup vinegar

4 tablespoons soy sauce

½ teaspoon hot sauce (or more to taste)

1 cup green pepper, cubed

½ cup red pepper, cubed

1 cup chopped onion

1. Season halibut cubes with salt and pepper and coat with flour. In a large skillet, sauté halibut in mixture of butter and oil for about 4 to 6 minutes or until browned. Remove and set aside.

2. Add water to reserved pineapple syrup to equal 2 cups. In a medium bowl, combine syrup/water mixture, sugar, and cornstarch and mix well. Stir in vinegar, soy sauce, and hot sauce.

3. In the same skillet, sauté peppers and onions for about 2 minutes or until crisp-tender. Add pineapple juice mixture to skillet and bring to a boil. Cook and stir for 2 minutes or until thickened. Add pineapple chunks and combine.

4. Remove from heat and fold in halibut. Pour into a large baking dish and bake at 350° F for 10 to 15 minutes. Serve over brown or white rice.

Nan's Notes: *All right, Nick and Amy spoiled us with Alaskan halibut from their fishing trips. If you don't have fresh or frozen halibut, this is great with chicken.*

Chef Mark Rubin's Rice Noodles Sichuan with Shrimp

MAKES 6 SERVINGS

(From our video recipe shoot at Second Harvest Food Bank)

12 ounces dried thin rice noodles

12 ounces of shrimp

MARINADE:

2 tablespoons oyster sauce

2 teaspoons white rice wine

2 teaspoons light soy sauce

1 teaspoon sesame oil

2 teaspoons cornstarch

1½ teaspoons sugar

1 teaspoon salt

Pinch of white pepper

TO PREPARE:

4½ to 5½ tablespoons canola oil

2 thin slices ginger, lightly smashed

4 ounces snow peas, ends and strings removed and finely julienned

1 head of baby bok choy, thinly sliced

¾ cup finely julienned red bell peppers

1 serrano chili, finely julienned (seeds removed)

4 scallions, cut into 2-inch lengths and white portions quartered lengthwise

2 garlic cloves, lightly smashed

½ teaspoon salt

1. Soak noodles in a bowl of hot water for 15 to 20 minutes to soften. Drain, stirring 2 or 3 times as they dry. Clean the shrimp and cut each shrimp in half lengthwise.

2. In a bowl, mix together all of the marinade ingredients. Add shrimp, turn to coat well, and let rest for 20 minutes.

3. Heat a wok over high heat for 30 seconds. Coat with 1 tablespoon of oil. When a wisp of smoke appears, add 1 ginger slice and stir for 45 seconds. Add the snow peas and bok choy and stir-fry for 20 seconds or until they turn bright green. Add the bell peppers, serrano chili, and scallions and stir-fry for 1½ minutes or until very hot. If too dry, sprinkle in some water. Transfer to a mixing bowl.

4. Coat the wok with 1½ tablespoons of oil. When a wisp of smoke appears, add the remaining ginger slice and garlic, and stir for 45 seconds or until the garlic releases its fragrance. Add the shrimp and marinade and spread in a single layer. Cook for 1 minute or until shrimp begins to turn pink. Transfer shrimp to mixing bowl.

5. Coat the wok with 2 tablespoons of oil. When a wisp of smoke appears, gently add the rice noodles to avoid splattering. Stir-fry for 1 minute, lower heat to medium, and stir-fry for 6 minutes more or until very hot.

6. If wok becomes dry, add remaining oil. Raise the heat to high, add shrimp and vegetables, and stir-fry together for 2 minutes or until well mixed. Transfer to plate and serve.

Chef Mark Rubin, the man behind the meals at First Harvest Café in Nashville.

Second Harvest

Second Harvest Food Bank of Middle Tennessee is a place I've gotten to know pretty well over the last few years because we've shot the *Top 20 Countdown* there several times. Its mission in this community is to feed hungry people and to help solve hunger issues. Last year alone, they helped collect and distribute over 28 million pounds of food to over 450 partner agencies. That translates to 20 million meals served to children, families, and seniors throughout the 46 counties it serves.

One way they raise funds to do this important work is with the First Harvest Café located in their Culinary Arts Center inside the Food Bank. Two days a week, you can go in, sit down to a lunch buffet, and know you're helping with their mission. I was fortunate to learn a delicious one-pan dish from the director of the center, Chef Mark Rubin. He's been a chef in Nashville for years and owned several restaurants. These days he's turned his successful career into a culinary mission. That's my kind of guy—a great chef with an even greater heart. Keep up the good work, Chef Mark and Second Harvest!

LUNCH & DINNER   121

Spicy Shrimp Casserole

MAKES 6–8 SERVINGS

Momma made this shrimp casserole for so many family dinners, and it's a special meal. Fresh shrimp at our house was like the ice cream truck coming down the road—we got all excited. My parents live so close to the Gulf Coast of Mississippi that they make regular trips down to the beach to load up on fresh shrimp. You know you're special if you come to my momma's house, and she serves you shrimp.

- 2 to 2½ pounds raw shrimp
- 9 tablespoons butter, divided
- 2 tablespoons liquid crab boil (I like Zatarain's)
- 1 cup chopped onion
- 1 cup chopped green bell pepper
- 1 cup chopped celery
- 2 garlic cloves, minced
- 1 (10¾-ounce) can cream of shrimp soup
- 1 (10¾-ounce) can Cheddar cheese soup
- ⅓ cup chopped parsley
- ½ cup chopped green onion with tops
- 2 cups cooked rice
- 1 teaspoon salt
- 1 teaspoon black pepper
- ¼ cup breadcrumbs

1. In a large, deep skillet, sauté shrimp in half of butter and crab boil. Drain shrimp and set aside on a plate, leaving juices in the pan.

2. To the same pan, add remaining butter and sauté onions, green bell pepper, celery, and garlic. Add soups, parsley, onion with tops and blend well. Stir in rice and salt and pepper.

3. Return shrimp to the pan, mix well and pour into a 3-quart casserole dish and sprinkle with breadcrumbs. Bake at 350° F for 30 minutes.

Nan's Notes: *If you don't like heat and I mean full-bodied heat, sauté the shrimp in only 1 tablespoon of the crab boil and go from there. Start small—you can always build up, but if you're like me, and heat is where it's at, then knock yourself out!*

Shrimp Casserole

MAKES 6–8 SERVINGS

I've got to have both shrimp casseroles represented here—mom's and mom-in-law's! I'm no dummy. If I get those ladies mad at me, then I'll be out some meals. These are similar recipes, but the heat factor is different and creates a different flavor. You be the judge. They BOTH win the Best Shrimp Casserole recipe contest. How's that for diplomacy.

¼ cup raw rice

1 (8-ounce) package cream cheese

1 stick butter

2 tablespoons butter

1 large onion, chopped

1 bell pepper, chopped

2 stalks celery, chopped

2 pounds raw shrimp (1 pound raw shrimp if including crabmeat)

1 (10¾-ounce) can cream of mushroom soup

1 (4-ounce) can mushrooms, drained

1 tablespoon garlic salt

1 teaspoon Tabasco sauce

1 pint crabmeat (optional)

Sharp grated cheese

Cracker crumbs

1. Cook rice according to package in medium saucepan. When rice is done, turn burner to warm and add cream cheese and butter to the pan. Cover and let sit.

2. In a large skillet on medium-high heat, melt 2 tablespoons butter and sauté onions, peppers, and celery until tender. Add in shrimp and cook until shrimp turn pink in color. Add soup, mushrooms, seasonings, and crabmeat (optional).

3. Remove lid from rice and stir well to blend. Add rice mixture to shrimp pan. Mix well and pour into a 2-quart casserole dish. Top with cheese and cracker crumbs. Bake at 350° F for 20 to 30 minutes.

South Mississippi Shrimp Creole

MAKES 6 SERVINGS

PREPARATION TIME: 20 MINUTES • COOKING TIME: 55 MINUTES

Sometimes food can be like a song. A certain dish can spark a moment in time just like a melody, and the next thing you know, you're walking down memory lane with every bite you take. Shrimp Creole does that for me. I remember sitting in my nannie's kitchen on North 30th Avenue in Hattiesburg, Mississippi, and eating this dish. I think she was also making pear preserves that day. It's funny how the mind works—I forget things that happened just a few years ago, but I can remember that day like it was last week. Thank goodness for memories like this that stay in your mind forever.

½ cup chopped onion

½ cup chopped celery

½ cup chopped green pepper

1 garlic clove, chopped

2 tablespoons oil

1 (14.5-ounce) can Red Gold® Petite Diced Tomatoes

1 (8-ounce) can Red Gold® Tomato Sauce

1½ teaspoons salt

1 teaspoon sugar

½ teaspoon chili powder

1 tablespoon Worcestershire sauce

Dash of Tabasco sauce

2 bay leaves

2 teaspoons cornstarch

4 teaspoons cold water

1 pound raw, peeled shrimp

½ cup chopped, fresh parsley

Hot cooked rice

1. In a large saucepan, sauté onions, celery, peppers, and garlic in oil until tender.

2. Add tomatoes, tomato sauce, salt, sugar, chili powder, Worcestershire sauce, Tabasco sauce, and bay leaves. Simmer for about 45 minutes.

3. Mix together cornstarch and cold water and add to sauce. Cook until thick. Add shrimp and parsley; simmer for 5 minutes or until shrimps are done. Remove bay leaves before serving. Serve over rice with hot, buttered garlic bread.

Nan and Nannie

If I had to name the one person in my life that made me aware of the importance of the presentation of food and the love that goes into not only making it taste great, but making it look great, too—it's my grandmother, Elsie Broome. Looking back now, even though I never actually cooked with her, the memories of what she cooked and the pride she took in displaying those amazing dishes are the blueprints I follow every time I set out to prepare a meal today. We lost her years ago, but there is not a day that goes by that I don't think of her.

When she passed away in 1993, my mother told my sister and me to pick a few things of hers to keep and remember her by. My sister chose a gold ring in the shape of a butterfly that Nannie always wore. Me? Well, ever the hungry one, I picked her recipe box. That little brown box with the multicolored rooster painted on the front sat on the counter in her kitchen for as long as I can remember. Filled with recipe cards written in her hand, receipts, newspaper and magazine clippings, and even the key to an old Ford

that she and Paw Paw Lonnie owned. It now sits on my kitchen counter with its contents unchanged. The multicolored rooster is still there too; slightly less vibrant due to the years of cooking that he oversaw. It needs to be cleaned, but I keep it as is because those small grease stains on the sides might be from the same oil that Nannie was frying okra or eggplant in, having leapt from a piping hot skillet to forever remain a part of the wood itself. There's surely some flour embedded in the hinges from where she closed the lid with white-coated hands after dredging chicken or minute steak. No, I can never clean it, there is too much of her that still remains on the box as well as in it.

I think she would be so pleased to know that the recipes in that box are guiding me now and that I'm sharing them here with you. And that her granddaughter, who has had the good fortune to travel the world, would rather be in the kitchen with that multicolored rooster than just about anywhere else.

Slow Cooker Pot Roast

MAKES 6–8 SERVINGS

Momma always put a roast on before we left for Sunday school, and when we came in from church, the smell would greet us at the door. It was just heavenly. This is my favorite way to cook a roast because it is hard to mess up and turns out perfectly every time. Slow cooking allows you to get the less expensive cuts of meat, and they tender up beautifully.

- 1 (4- to 5-pound) beef roast (I like bottom round)
- 2 tablespoons canola or vegetable oil for browning
- Flour to coat
- 1 jumbo garlic clove (or 2 large cloves), peeled and chopped into 5 to 7 pieces
- Salt and freshly ground black pepper
- Garlic powder
- ½ cup dry red wine
- 1 tablespoon prepared horseradish
- 1 tablespoon brown sugar
- 1 teaspoon Dijon mustard
- 1 bay leaf
- 3 or 4 stalks of celery, chopped
- 5 to 7 peeled carrots, cut into large pieces
- 4 or 5 peeled potatoes, cut into large pieces
- 1 large onion, cut into medium pieces

1. Rinse roast and pat dry with a paper towel. Heat oil in slow cooker pan on medium-high on the stovetop (make sure your pan is stovetop safe).

2. Coat all sides of roast with flour. Make a couple of slits with a knife into each side of roast and insert garlic pieces. Brown roast in the slow cooker pan on each side until light brown, seasoning each side with salt, pepper, and garlic powder as you go. Carefully drain off oil, transfer slow cooker pan to its hot plate, and turn heat to medium-high.

3. Mix wine, horseradish, brown sugar, and mustard in a small bowl and pour over roast. Drop in bay leaf. Cover and cook for two hours.

4. Remove lid and place celery around roast, followed by carrots, potatoes, and onions—reserving a couple of onion pieces for the top of the roast. Season vegetables with salt and pepper. Cover and depending on the size of roast, cook for an additional 4 to 5 hours or until roast is done. Remove bay leaf before serving.

Jay Lane serving up my favorite new way to make meat loaf.

Canadian Cooking in a Country Kitchen

When I first moved to Nashville, I was a waitress at a wonderful restaurant called The Cooker. I lived off their homemade rolls and chicken tenders with honey mustard sauce, and they made a mean meat loaf, too. Their version was just about my favorite until I met Jay Lane.

Jay is a medium from Sudbury, Ontario, and I was so glad to meet her when she visited Nashville and even more glad that she agreed to come to the house and show me how to put a Canadian twist on a quintessential American classic. This is a recipe I had never heard of, but one that left an impression. I made this dish three times within two weeks after Jay introduced me to it. Easy and impressive looking on your table.

Meat Loaf Wellington

MAKES 6–8 SERVINGS

(From our video recipe shoot with medium Jay Lane)

- 1 egg lightly beaten
- 1 cup spaghetti sauce (no meat added)
- ¼ cup dry breadcrumbs
- ½ teaspoon salt
- ¼ teaspoon black pepper
- 1½ pounds ground beef
- 2 cups shredded low fat mozzarella cheese
- ½ tablespoon fresh minced parsley
- 1 (8-ounce) tube refrigerated crescent rolls

1. In a large bowl, combine the egg, ⅓ cup spaghetti sauce, breadcrumbs, salt, and pepper. Crumble in beef and mix well.

2. On a piece of heavy-duty foil, pat beef mixture into a rectangle about 12 x 8 inches. Sprinkle 1 cup cheese and parsley on top to within 1 inch of edges. Roll up jellyroll style, starting with the long side and peel foil away while rolling. Seal seam and ends.

3. Place seam side down in a greased 9 x 13-inch baking dish. Bake uncovered at 350° F for about one hour. Drain the drippings.

4. Unroll crescent dough and seal seams and perforations. Drape dough over meat loaf to cover the top, sides, and ends; seal ends. Or you can separate pieces and drape the triangles (slightly overlapping) on top of the loaf.

5. Bake 15 to 20 minutes longer or until crust is golden brown. Let stand for 5 minutes before serving. Carefully transfer meat loaf to a serving platter using a spatula. Sprinkle with remaining cheese. Serve with remaining spaghetti sauce, if desired.

LUNCH & DINNER

Miss Pat's Spaghetti Sauce

MAKES 4–6 SERVINGS

Returning from the first book because it is the preferred spaghetti sauce at our house. Miss Pat got this one from her mother-in-law, so it's appropriate that I got it from her. This version uses tomato soup—a very different spin on sauce. It's not a traditional tasting Italian marinara-type sauce, but it's hearty, filling, and extra good!

6 bacon slices

1 pound ground beef

2 garlic cloves, minced

1 small onion, chopped

1 small green pepper, chopped

2 (10¾-ounce) cans condensed tomato soup

1 (4-ounce) can mushrooms, drained (optional)

Cooked spaghetti

Parmesan cheese

1. Fry bacon in a deep skillet until crisp. Remove, crumble, and set aside. To the same skillet, add ground beef, garlic, onion, and green pepper and brown well. Add bacon and tomato soup to meat mixture and blend well. Simmer slowly on low for 2 to 4 hours.

2. If desired, add the mushrooms about 30 minutes before serving. Serve over hot cooked spaghetti with freshly grated Parmesan cheese on top.

Nan's Notes: *Miss Pat transfers the sauce mixture to a double boiler for simmering, but I just simmer in the same pot…of course I do! This sauce can be frozen, and it's nice to have a batch of it ready to thaw and use when needed.*

Mushroom-Stuffed Ravioli Sauté

MAKES 4 SERVINGS

This is in the top three of my favorite one-pan entrées. It is pretty darn delicious and impressive, with ingredients that aren't typical—pears, Gorgonzola cheese, and chicken sausage. This is definitely "company worthy."

- 2 tablespoons olive oil
- 3 links (6 ounces) chicken (or pork) Italian sausage, cut into bite-sized pieces (I like the kind with peppers in it)
- 8 ounces baby portabella mushrooms, sliced
- 1 cup chopped plus ½ cup grated Bartlett pear
- 1 cup white wine (or chicken stock)
- ½ pound fresh asparagus spears, ends removed and cut into 2-inch pieces
- ½ teaspoon garlic powder
- 1 teaspoon dried basil
- 1 (8-ounce) package cheese-filled ravioli with mushrooms
- 4 ounces crumbled Gorgonzola cheese
- ½ teaspoon freshly ground black pepper

1. Preheat large sauté pan on medium-high for 2 to 3 minutes. Place oil in pan and then add sausage. Cook 5 to 7 minutes or until browned.

2. Add in portabella mushrooms and cook for 2 to 3 minutes, stirring often. Add chopped pear and sauté one minute. Reduce heat to medium.

3. Stir in wine, grated pear, asparagus, garlic powder, basil, and pasta. Simmer 4 to 5 minutes or until pasta is tender and wine has cooked down a little more than half.

4. Remove pan from heat. Stir in cheese until blended. Sprinkle with pepper and serve.

Clara

When Charlie and I got married, we bought a little ranch-style house with a big backyard in a Nashville neighborhood called Donelson. Charlie quickly went about the business of building a split rail fence lined with wire to keep our pups Molly and Bailey safe in their own yard, and that's how we met our new neighbors, Cliff and Clara Ward. Cliff showed us where the property lines were and Clara soon became my friend and my cooking buddy.

Originally from Kentucky, Clara is steeped in southern cooking culture just like all my family and friends back home, and she has a cookbook collection that even Julia Child would have envied! With all her experience and knowledge, she can usually tell whether a recipe is going to be good just by reading the ingredients. As I got more serious in the kitchen, I would run things by her to see what she thought. If I doubted her and tried a recipe anyway, I usually regretted it—probably not as much as Charlie though! Eventually I learned my lesson and started to recognize the recipes that were best suited to my taste buds a little quicker. As I progressed, I tried new things and Clara was my taste tester. Once again, she could tell almost immediately if the recipe would be better with a little more of this and a little less of that...and she was always right.

With Clara on the set of "Talk of the Town." She went with me that day to help out... I couldn't ask for a better sous chef!

Over the years, Cliff and Clara have become like parents to us. When we lived next door to them, I knew that if I ever needed anything, all I had to do was walk across the driveway and knock, and just like my own mother, she'd always be there for me. An old Jewish proverb says, "God could not be everywhere and therefore he made mothers." God must have known I would need a lot of watching because He gave me several mothers in Hattiesburg. I guess He knew I would need watching in Nashville too, and gave the job to Clara.

Sweet & Sour Beef with Vegetables

MAKES 6 SERVINGS

This is one from Clara, and it's my favorite way to cook—in the slow cooker.

- 2 pounds round or chuck steak, cut in 1-inch cubes
- 2 tablespoons vegetable oil
- 2 (8-ounce) cans tomato sauce
- 1 teaspoon salt
- ½ cup vinegar
- ½ cup light molasses
- 2 cups carrots, sliced ¼-inch thick
- 2 cups small, white onions, peeled
- 2 teaspoons chili powder
- 2 teaspoons paprika
- ¼ cup sugar
- 1 large green bell pepper, cut into 1-inch squares
- 1 medium red bell pepper, cut into 1-inch squares
- Shell macaroni, cooked
- Fresh chives, for garnish

1. Heat oil in the slow cooker pan on the stovetop and brown steak (ensure that your pan is safe for the stovetop). If not, brown steak in a sauté pan and transfer to slow cooker pan.

2. Add all remaining ingredients, mix well, and move pan to the base of the slow cooker. Cook 6 to 7 hours on low or 3 to 4 hours on high.

3. Serve with cooked shell macaroni and garnish with chives.

Italian Sausage Manicotti

MAKES 8 SERVINGS

I go back for seconds on this one, but I guess I do that with most everything! Pair this with the Bruschetta appetizer (recipe on page 30), and you've got a delicious Italian meal for company or any night of the week.

3 cups ricotta cheese

¾ cup freshly grated Parmesan cheese, divided

¼ cup shredded mozzarella cheese

2 eggs, lightly beaten

3 tablespoons chopped fresh parsley

2 tablespoons Italian seasoning

1½ teaspoons garlic powder

½ teaspoon crushed red pepper flakes

½ teaspoon salt

½ teaspoon black pepper

1 pound Italian sausage, casing removed

1 (28-ounce) can crushed tomatoes in puree, undrained

1 (24-ounce) jar marinara or spaghetti sauce

8 ounces uncooked manicotti noodles

1. In a large bowl, mix together ricotta cheese, ½ cup Parmesan cheese, mozzarella cheese, eggs, parsley, Italian seasoning, garlic powder, red pepper flakes, salt, and black pepper and set aside.

2. In a large skillet over medium-high heat, cook sausage until brown, stirring well to crumble. When done, remove sausage from skillet and lay on paper towels to drain. Remove drippings from skillet.

3. To the same skillet, add tomatoes and marinara or spaghetti sauce and simmer for about 5 or 10 minutes.

4. Spray a 9 x 13-inch baking pan with nonstick cooking spray. Pour about ⅓ of sauce into pan. Add sausage to remaining sauce. Stuff each noodle with about ½ cup cheese mixture and place in dish on top of sauce. Top noodles with tomato sauce.

5. Cover tightly with foil and bake at 375° F for 50 minutes to 1 hour or until noodles are cooked. Cool for about 5 minutes before serving. Sprinkle remaining Parmesan cheese on top and serve

Nan's Notes: *You can make up both the sauce and the cheese mixture ahead of time, and put it together when you're ready to bake it.*

One Pan Beef Stroganoff

MAKES 8 SERVINGS

Awhile back, I had a great day in the kitchen cooking this dish with my friend Clara. I wanted her to taste it and give me her opinion. We both agreed—this is perfect comfort food for the one you love on a cold night.

3 tablespoons butter, divided

8 ounces mushrooms, sliced

1 cup chopped onion

1 garlic clove, minced

1 pound beef sirloin, cut into thin strips

3 tablespoons flour

1½ teaspoons paprika

¼ cup dry red wine

4 cups beef broth

¾ teaspoon salt

½ teaspoon freshly ground black pepper

8 ounces uncooked egg noodles

½ cup sour cream

Chopped parsley for garnish

1. In a large Dutch oven over medium-high, heat up 1 tablespoon butter and add in mushrooms. Sauté for about 5 minutes. Remove mushrooms from pan and set aside.

2. Lower the heat to medium and add in remaining butter. Cook onions and garlic for about 4 to 5 minutes.

3. Place the beef in the pan and sauté for about 6 to 8 minutes. Sprinkle in flour and paprika and stir well to coat meat. Cook for an additional 1 to 2 minutes, stirring occasionally.

4. Pour in wine and stir well. Simmer for about 1 to 2 minutes, allowing wine to mostly evaporate. Pour in the broth, add in salt and pepper, and stir to combine. Adjust the heat to medium-high and simmer for a couple of minutes.

5. Add in the noodles and the mushrooms and stir to combine. Reduce heat and simmer for about 6 to 7 minutes or until noodles are tender.

6. Remove pan from the heat and stir in the sour cream. Season to taste with salt and pepper and serve with chopped parsley on top.

Nan's Notes: *Make sure to get good beef AND good wine. If the wine is not good enough to drink by the glass, don't cook with it either.*

One Pan Tex-Mex Pasta

MAKES 6 SERVINGS

PREPARATION TIME: 15 MINUTES • COOKING TIME: 30 MINUTES

This recipe is a collision of my two dominant food cravings that happened on the same day—pasta and Mexican food. It's a perfect storm of flavors and a combination that had me going back for seconds and wanting thirds. A one-pan, stick-to-your-ribs skillet dinner that's not typical with plenty of liquid for the spaghetti to cook right in the same pot.

- 1 pound ground beef
- 1 medium onion, chopped
- Canola or vegetable oil (for browning)
- 1 teaspoon cumin
- ½ teaspoon chili powder
- 1 teaspoon salt
- 1 (8-ounce) can Red Gold® Tomato Sauce
- 1 (10-ounce) can Red Gold® Petite Diced Tomatoes & Green Chilies
- 2 cups Red Gold® Salsa
- 3 cups Red Gold® No Salt Added Tomato Juice
- 1 (15-ounce) can pinto beans, drained
- 1 (11-ounce) can shoepeg corn
- 8 ounces Fideo pasta (cut spaghetti)
- ½ cup freshly grated Cheddar cheese, plus more for garnish
- Sour cream
- Fresh chopped cilantro

1. In a large Dutch oven, brown ground beef and onion in a little bit of oil on medium-high heat. Once browned, season with cumin, chili powder, and salt.

2. Pour in tomato sauce, tomatoes, salsa, and tomato juice and stir to combine. Add in pinto beans, corn, and pasta and stir to blend. Turn heat to low, put the lid on, and cook for about 20 to 30 minutes or until pasta is tender and most of the juice has absorbed. Make sure heat is low and stir a couple of times to prevent sticking.

3. Once done, sprinkle Cheddar cheese on top and return lid for a couple of minutes to melt cheese. Top each serving with more Cheddar cheese (if desired), sour cream, and cilantro.

Nan's Notes: *Serve with guacamole and tortilla chips for a perfect Mexi-talian meal.*

LUNCH & DINNER

Chicken Stroganoff

MAKES 6–8 SERVINGS

(From our video recipe shoot with Jamie O'Neal)

You've got to love someone that will ask you to stay for dinner after you've just invaded their kitchen with a camera crew for the bulk of the day. That's why I love Jamie O'Neal!

She's had back to back number one singles on country radio with "There Is No Arizona" and "When I Think About Angels." She's Grammy-nominated, and she's one of the best singers in any genre of music. This dish is something Jamie, her husband Rod, and their talented daughter Aliyah all love, and after sitting down with a plateful, I can certainly taste why.

Olive oil for sautéing

1 large onion, diced

2 heaping tablespoons minced garlic

2 packages chicken tenders (about 2 pounds), cut into pieces

½ stick butter

Sea salt to taste

White pepper to taste

½ (24-ounce) container low fat sour cream

¼ to ½ cup red wine

1 large pack fresh whole mushrooms, stems removed, peeled and sliced

Hot cooked rice

1. Heat a little olive oil in a large sauté pan on medium-high. Add onions and garlic and cook until tender, about 5 to 6 minutes.

2. Add in chicken and cook until brown on both sides, stirring often. May add a little more oil if needed for browning. Once chicken has browned, add in butter and stir to melt.

3. Lower heat to simmer and season with salt and white pepper to taste. Add in sour cream and simmer for a few minutes.

4. Pour in red wine, starting with a ¼ cup and adding more if desired. Stir in the mushrooms and simmer on low heat until the mushrooms are soft and the sauce has thickened. Serve over hot, cooked white rice.

There may be "No Arizona," but there sure is some good cooking going on in Jamie O'Neal's kitchen…

…and a whole lot of fun, too!

LUNCH & DINNER

Chicken Parmesan Lasagna

MAKES 12 SERVINGS

PREPARATION TIME: 25 MINUTES • COOKING TIME: 1 HOUR

(From my video recipe shoot with Selita Reichart of Red Gold Tomatoes)

- 5 thin-cut boneless skinless chicken breasts or 1½ pounds chicken tenders
- 2 tablespoons all-purpose flour
- 2 eggs, beaten
- 3 cups panko bread crumbs
- 1 cup grated Parmesan cheese
- ½ cup extra virgin olive oil
- 1 (28-ounce) can Red Gold® Crushed Tomatoes or 2 (15-ounce) cans Red Gold® Crushed Tomatoes
- 2 (14.5-ounce) cans Red Gold® Diced Tomatoes with Basil, Garlic & Oregano
- ½ cup water
- 1 teaspoon Italian seasoning
- Salt to taste
- 1 (16-ounce) box traditional lasagna noodles, uncooked
- 1 (15-ounce) carton low fat ricotta cheese
- 3 cups (16 ounces) shredded mozzarella cheese
- ½ cup grated Parmesan cheese
- ¼ cup chopped fresh basil

Nan's Notes: *Divide the recipe into two 9 x 9-inch baking dishes and freeze one for a wintry night supper.*

1. Preheat oven to 350° F. Place flour in a sifter or strainer. Place chicken breasts on a piece of foil and sprinkle with flour from the sifter, on both sides. Place beaten eggs into a shallow bowl. Mix breadcrumbs and ½ cup Parmesan cheese in a separate bowl.

2. Dip chicken breasts in beaten eggs, then breadcrumb mixture, pressing crumbs into both sides. Repeat with each breast. Heat oil in a large skillet over medium high heat. Cook chicken until golden, about 2 minutes on each side. Cool and cube chicken to use as a layer in the lasagna

3. In a large mixing bowl, combine crushed tomatoes, diced tomatoes, water, Italian seasoning, and salt. Stir until ingredients are thoroughly combined.

4. Cover the bottom of a 9 x 13-inch baking pan with 1½ cups of sauce mixture. Arrange ⅓ of noodles on top of sauce, slightly overlapped. Top with ½ of ricotta cheese, ⅓ cubed chicken, 1 cup of mozzarella cheese, and 1 cup of sauce. Repeat layers and top with last ⅓ of noodles, the remaining sauce, and the last ⅓ cubed chicken. Sprinkle with remaining mozzarella and Parmesan cheese.

5. Cover tightly with foil and bake for 1 to 1½ hours until noodles are cooked. If you prefer the cheese on top of lasagna to be crispy, remove foil the last 10 minutes of cooking time. Let stand for 15 minutes before serving. Sprinkle top with fresh chopped basil before serving.

In the kitchen of Selita Reichart of Red Gold Tomatoes

Tomato Country

I've been a customer of Red Gold Tomatoes for a long time. So, when I had the opportunity to travel up to Elwood, Indiana, to visit and cook with the folks who produce my favorite canned tomatoes, I couldn't get Charlie and cameraman Mark Mitchell in the Toyota fast enough! I joke in the video that my tomato shelf in my pantry is sagging because I've got it stocked full of Red Gold tomatoes, but it's true. They simply taste great, and I especially appreciate what it says on the label—made with pride and care by the same Midwestern family since 1942. That's the reason I started buying them to begin with.

And what a good time we had up in tomato country. Selita Reichart, who owns the company with her husband Brian, invited me into her kitchen for some good conversation and a great-tasting recipe—**Chicken Parmesan Lasagna**, made of course with Red Gold Tomatoes. Thank you, Selita and Red Gold!

LUNCH & DINNER

Chicken in a Basket

MAKES 8 SERVINGS

I love crescent rolls. I love to pop the tube, unroll the dough, and almost instantly end up with a warm, flakey treat begging for a little butter. During a six day iced-in retreat in Nashville one recent winter, I came up with this recipe, ran it past my ace taste-tester, Charlie, and we both gave it the thumbs up. It's just the kind of dish I like—uptown on the outside and down-home on the inside.

1 cup chopped mushrooms

1 cup chopped onions

2 tablespoons olive oil

2 chicken breasts, finely chopped

2 tablespoons Tone's Rosemary Garlic seasoning

Salt and freshly ground black pepper to taste

3 tablespoons chopped pimento (reserve some juice from the jar)

½ cup frozen peas

4 ounces cream cheese, cut into 4 or 5 pieces

2 tubes (8 rolls each) refrigerated crescent rolls

Nan's Notes: *The pimento gives it a classic zing. Add a green vegetable and you're good to go. Make sure the point ends don't all stick together when twisting the top together. Try to separate them so that each point is laid out and looking pretty!*

1. In a medium skillet, sauté mushrooms and onions in 1 tablespoon olive oil until soft. Remove from the pan when done and set aside.

2. Add remaining olive oil to the pan and heat up. Place chicken in the skillet, sprinkle with Rosemary Garlic seasoning, and stir to blend. Sauté on medium heat until done, stirring often for even browning. Season with salt and pepper.

3. When chicken is done, add the onions and mushrooms back to pan and pour in pimento and peas. Stir to blend and heat through. Drop in cream cheese and cover. Turn heat to low.

4. While cream cheese is melting, unroll crescent rolls and tear off at the main perforations, leaving the two triangle pieces attached. Lay each square piece individually onto a baking sheet and pinch perforations to seal.

5. Stir chicken mixture to blend melted cream cheese. If mixture is dry, moisten with a little reserved pimento juice. If mixture is too wet, leave the lid off and simmer for a few minutes.

6. Place 2 to 3 heaping tablespoons of filling into the center of a square. Pull up all four corners together, while gently pressing the shorter side seams together so that none of the filling bubbles out. Gently twist while holding all 4 sides so that the top holds together. Bake at 375° F for 10 to 12 minutes or until dough is golden brown.

LUNCH & DINNER 143

Chicken Jambalaya

MAKES 12–14 SERVINGS

(From our video recipe shoot with Robert St. John)

- 2 pounds Andouille sausage (or any mild smoked pork sausage link), sliced about ¼-inch thick
- 3 pounds chicken thigh meat, boneless and skinless, cut into 1½-inch pieces
- 1 tablespoon Creole seasoning
- 2 cups yellow onion, medium diced
- 1½ cups celery, medium diced
- 1½ cups green bell pepper, medium diced
- 2 tablespoons fresh garlic, minced
- 1 teaspoon dried thyme
- 3 bay leaves
- 1 pound long grain rice
- 1 (14-ounce) can diced tomatoes
- 1 tablespoon Worcestershire sauce
- 1 tablespoon hot sauce
- 1 quart + 1 cup chicken broth, heated
- 1 tablespoon kosher salt

1. Heat a large heavy-duty cast iron skillet or Dutch oven (2 gallon capacity) on high heat. Place the sausage in the hot skillet and brown it evenly. Stir often to prevent burning. When the sausage is browned, carefully remove the excess fat.

2. Season the chicken with the Creole seasoning and add it to the skillet. Brown the chicken evenly and cook for 20 minutes.

3. Add in onion, celery, and bell pepper and lower the heat to medium. Cook for 10 minutes, stirring often.

4. Add in the garlic, thyme, and bay leaves and cook for 5 more minutes.

5. Stir in the rice and cook until the grains are hot. Add in canned tomatoes, Worcestershire sauce, hot sauce, and chicken broth. Stir the mixture well to prevent rice from clumping together. Lower the heat until the jambalaya is just barely simmering and cover. Cook for 30 minutes.

Jokes and jambalaya make for a good day in the kitchen with Robert St. John.

Culinary Humanitarian

Robert St. John is a three-time winner of "Best Chef in Mississippi." He's written 10 books, has 5 restaurants (Crescent City Grill, Purple Parrot Café, Branch, Tabella, and Mahogany Bar) and is gearing up for a sixth! I first met Robert when I was in college, and he hired me as a server at Crescent City Grill. It was one of the best jobs I've ever had.

When we started One Pan Nan, he was at the top of my list to shoot a video recipe with, and that's when I learned who Robert St. John really is. Like me, he's never met a stranger. He's lively, fun, and outgoing, and of course, he knows his way around the kitchen. What makes Robert so special is not only his personality and love for the cuisine of the region, but his concern for the community and his home state. In 2009, Robert started Extra Table, a non-profit organization that provides food pantries and soup kitchens with the food they need. Shipping healthy food bundles by the ton to these agencies, Robert is helping fight hunger all over Mississippi, and in Hattiesburg alone, his philanthropic efforts help feed over 1,200 people every month through the Edwards Street Fellowship Center.

Having a taste for great food and a heart for feeding the hungry makes Robert St. John a man that the state of Mississippi can add to its long lineage of talented people and great humanitarians. I'm proud to know him and honored to have him represented in this book. Next time you're in Hattiesburg, stop by one of his restaurants and say hello—I bet you'll walk out with a full belly and a new friend.

Thyme & Shallots Chicken

MAKES 4 SERVINGS

I think you can gauge how good a recipe is by how worn and stained the recipe card is. I can't tell you how many years I've been making this dish, but the card has seen better days as it's now tattered, torn, and splattered with butter and flour—signs of a well-loved recipe! It looks like it was cooked in three different pans, but it's truly all in one pan, and all of those flavors come together to make up the most delicious sauce at the end.

- 4 tablespoons butter
- 2 thick boneless chicken breasts, filleted into 2 pieces each
- 2 tablespoons flour
- Salt and freshly ground black pepper
- 4 shallots, diced
- 1 teaspoon minced garlic
- 1 cup peeled and diced red potatoes
- 1 cup chicken broth
- 1 tablespoon dried thyme
- 6 ounces fresh green beans, trimmed

1. In a large skillet, melt 2 tablespoons of butter over medium heat. Coat chicken fillets in flour and season with salt and pepper to taste. Cook chicken until brown, about 3 minutes for each side, flipping only once. Remove chicken from pan and set aside.

2. To the same pan, add 1 tablespoon butter and sauté shallots and garlic for about 1 minute. Return chicken to pan and add potatoes, broth, and thyme. Season with salt and pepper, bring to a boil, and reduce heat to a simmer. Cover and cook until chicken is almost done, about 5 or 6 minutes.

3. Lay in the green beans, cover, and cook until chicken is done, about 2 or 3 more minutes. Transfer chicken and vegetables to plates, leaving as much juice in the pan as you can.

4. Cook and stir until sauce thickens and is smooth, adding remaining butter if needed. Pour sauce over chicken, and serve.

Nan's Notes: *If you don't have shallots, just use a white or red onion or green onions work great too.*

With country crooner Katie Armiger

Cooking with Katie

I've had the pleasure of interviewing country artist and Texas native Katie Armiger several times, and I just love being around her! I bet I have said her name more than a hundred times on the *Top 20 Countdown* because fans love her videos. One of them being "Safe"—it has over 2 million views on YouTube!

On top of being talented, she is one of the nicest and most approachable people. She was kind enough to come out to the house and do a little one-pan cooking with me, and she brought along this fabulous recipe. We cooked it up, and I honestly had to hold back and leave some on the plate for the cameras to film. It is that good!

Chicken with Pesto Cream Sauce

MAKES 2 SERVINGS

(From our video recipe shoot with recording artist Katie Armiger)

1 large chicken breast, filleted (or two smaller ones)

Sea salt

2 to 3 tablespoons flour

4 slices prosciutto

1 bunch asparagus, ends cut off and chopped into 2-inch pieces

2 tablespoons olive oil

½ cup half-and-half

⅓ cup pesto (recipe on page 35, or use store bought)

1 tablespoon Parmesan cheese shavings

Freshly ground black pepper

Freshly grated Parmesan cheese shavings (if desired)

Basil leaves for garnish

1. Rinse chicken, pat dry with a paper towel, and sprinkle both sides with sea salt. Coat each piece with flour and wrap each in 2 slices of prosciutto. Set aside.

2. Steam asparagus in a steamer basket, cooking for 5 minutes or until asparagus is tender. Transfer the asparagus to a bowl of ice water to stop the cooking. Leave for one minute, remove from water, and lay asparagus on a towel to drain.

3. In a large sauté pan, heat olive oil and add prepared chicken breasts. Cook on each side for about 6 minutes (or until chicken is no longer pink in the middle), flipping only once.

4. Pour in half-and-half, add the pesto and measured Parmesan cheese, and mix gently. Add the asparagus, turn up the heat, and let mixture reach a boil (the sauce should thicken slightly).

5. Turn off heat and season with sea salt and freshly ground black pepper if needed. Serve with Parmesan cheese shavings and basil garnish.

Green Curry Chicken

MAKES 4–6 SERVINGS

Curry, red or green, is my favorite dish to order at a Thai restaurant. I love that the rice soaks up all of that spicy, creamy coconut milk—simply wonderful! Cooking curry at home is not that complicated, and it's just as good as going out. Once you add a few of the staple ingredients for making good Thai food to the pantry, it is easy to do.

4 chicken breasts, cut into small pieces

1 can unsweetened coconut milk

3 garlic cloves, crushed

1 teaspoon Thai fish sauce (optional)

2 tablespoons Thai green curry paste

1 red pepper, sliced

1 green pepper, sliced

½ to 1 cup frozen or fresh peas

3 whole green chilies, diced or 1 (4-ounce) can diced green chilies

4 tablespoons chopped fresh cilantro

Salt and freshly ground black pepper to taste

Hot cooked basmati rice

Chopped fresh cilantro, for garnish

1. Shake coconut milk can very well. Pour coconut milk in a medium skillet and bring to a boil.

2. Drop in chicken, garlic, and fish oil (if using). Lower the heat and simmer for 30 minutes or until chicken has cooked. Stir occasionally.

3. When done, remove the chicken from the pan with a slotted spoon. Set aside and keep warm. Stir in the green curry paste to the coconut milk mixture. Then add peppers, peas, and chilies and simmer for about 5 or 10 minutes.

4. Return the chicken back to the pan and bring to a boil. Add salt and pepper to taste and stir in cilantro.

5. Serve over hot, cooked rice garnished with cilantro.

KK's Chicken Casserole

MAKES 6 SERVINGS

I can't count the times I have happily eaten this casserole at Miss Pat's. To really do it right, you have to use Utz brand potato chips out of Pennsylvania—the preferred chip on the Kelley farm!

- 2 cups diced cooked chicken
- 1½ cups diced celery
- ½ cup slivered almonds
- ½ teaspoon salt
- ½ teaspoon grated onion
- ¼ teaspoon pepper
- 2 tablespoons lemon juice
- 1 cup mayonnaise
- ½ cup grated sharp Cheddar cheese
- ⅔ cup crushed potato chips

1. Mix all ingredients together, except the potato chips, in a large bowl. Pour into a 9 x 9-inch or a 10 x 10-inch baking pan and sprinkle potato chips on the top. Bake at 375° F for 20 minutes.

Nan's Notes: *If you have any wheat allergies, this is gluten free. Add a veggie or a salad and you're done.*

Dutch Chicken

MAKES 6 SERVINGS

This continues to be a favorite here at home. Never fails, always good, and easy to make. As far as the name goes, you should know that we named it Dutch Chicken—though it is not Dutch at all nor does it have anything to do with anyone named Dutch or anyone in the Netherlands for that matter. It's a secret that I can't reveal because I can't remember…that's not exactly true, but it's as good a little white lie as any!

3 chicken breasts

1½ teaspoons garlic powder

1 teaspoon salt

1 large jar thick salsa

2 (15-ounce) cans black beans, drained and rinsed

1 (15¼-ounce) can kernel corn (drained)

1 teaspoon cumin

1 (4-ounce) can diced green chilies

1 (8-ounce) package cream cheese, cut into 1-inch pieces

1. Season chicken with garlic powder and salt. Place chicken in slow cooker or crockpot and pour remaining ingredients (except the cream cheese) on top. Do not stir.

2. Cover, set slow cooker to high, and cook for 1½ to 2 hours or until chicken is no longer pink inside.

3. Use two forks to shred chicken in the cooker. Drop in cream cheese pieces and blend thoroughly to melt.

4. Serve over tortilla chips, in a taco salad shell with lettuce, or atop cooked rice.

Nan's Notes: *Be sure to use a thick and chunky salsa—if you use a thinner one, it might make it too soupy.*

LUNCH & DINNER 153

Chicken Casserole

MAKES 8–10 SERVINGS

(From our video recipe shoot with the firefighters of Nashville Station 29)

- 6 boneless, skinless chicken breasts
- 1 (10¾-ounce) can cream of chicken soup
- 1 (10¾-ounce) can cream of mushroom soup
- 1 (8-ounce) container sour cream
- 2 sleeves Ritz crackers
- 1 stick butter, melted

1. In a large stockpot, boil chicken breasts until no longer pink in the middle and drain. Place chicken in a large bowl and cool for a few minutes.

2. Shred chicken with hands or use 2 forks. Pour in soups and sour cream and mix well.

3. Crush crackers while still in sleeves and sprinkle one sleeve on the bottom of a large baking pan. Spread chicken mixture on top of crackers in pan and sprinkle remaining sleeve of crackers on top.

4. Pour melted butter evenly all over casserole and bake at 350° F until bubbly hot, about 30 to 45 minutes.

With Engineer Tracy Townsend, Captain David Tomlinson, Firefighter Cody Evans and Engineer Bubba White.

Cookin' and cuttin' up in the kitchen with Engineer Tracy and Captain David—aka "Opie"

Breaking Bread with the Best

I have been blessed to do some pretty cool things in my career, and spending the afternoon with some of Nashville's first responders was a pleasure and an honor. I've always appreciated what our first responders do, but seeing first hand how alert and aware they are at all times and how quickly they react confirms that we are in good hands.

When they're on duty, the fire hall is their home away from home, and they spend a third of their lives at the station—24 hours at a time. So cooking a meal for a hungry crew that satisfies a variety of palates is a kitchen skill firefighters learn quickly.

Captain David Tomlinson shared this dish, his mom's Chicken Casserole. It's one of the favorites at Station 29, and it just might become one of yours too. I thank them for watching out for this community, for letting me break bread with them, and for sharing some wonderful food!

One Crust Chicken Pot Pie

MAKES 6 SERVINGS

(From our video recipe shoot with singer/songwriter Linda Davis)

⅓ cup butter

½ cup Bisquick

½ cup chopped onion

½ teaspoon black pepper

⅛ teaspoon dried thyme

1½ cups chicken broth

⅔ cup Carnation milk

1¾ cups boiled or roasted chicken (or turkey), cut up

2 (15-ounce) cans Veg-All, drained

CRUST:

1½ cups Bisquick

3 tablespoons hot water

3 tablespoons butter, softened

1. Heat oven to 425° F. Melt butter in a 2-quart saucepan over low heat. Stir in Bisquick, onion, pepper, and thyme. Cook over low heat, stirring constantly, until mixture is bubbly. Remove from heat.

2. Stir in chicken broth and milk. Heat to a boil, stirring constantly. Add chicken and Veg-All and heat through. Keep warm while mixing up crust.

3. Mix together Bisquick, hot water, and softened butter to form dough. Dust wax paper or cutting board with Bisquick and turn out dough onto it. Work dough and roll it out to fit the size of the small casserole dish you are using. (Linda and I used a pie plate.)

4. Pour chicken mixture into the butter-greased casserole dish and lay rolled-out dough on top. Cut a couple of slits in the dough or make holes with a fork for steam. Bake until crust is brown.

Grammy winner Linda Davis with her family-winning chicken pot pie.

Genuine Talent—
On & Off the Stage

You'd be hard pressed to find a sweeter, more genuine person than Linda Davis. If you're a country music fan, you know her voice from her Grammy-winning duet with Reba McEntire on the number one hit song "Does He Love You." If you're not a country fan, you've probably still heard her voice on commercial jingles for Kentucky Fried Chicken and Dr. Pepper. She's had 15 singles at radio, played sold out shows with Garth Brooks, George Strait, and Kenny Rogers, and raised two beautiful girls—Riley and Hillary—with her husband Lang Scott. Hillary follows in her mom's footsteps as one third of the hit trio Lady Antebellum.

How Linda can do all of that and still have skill in the kitchen is beyond me—this Texas gal can cook! Her Chicken Pot Pie is a family favorite that her girls grew up on, and it's the definition of hearty and delicious comfort food that's sure to satisfy. These days when Linda is not on the road singing or in the kitchen cooking, she helps up and coming entertainers find their comfort zone on the stage through her business called Stage Performance 101.

One Pan Chicken & Greens

MAKES 6 SERVINGS

This little casserole has nothing but all stars in it—chicken, bacon, greens, rice. You could use collard greens, mustard greens, or kale in this dish. Kale seems to be the "it" green right now, but I'll always be a good ole collards girl.

½ teaspoon salt

1 teaspoon smoked sweet paprika

½ teaspoon black pepper

6 skinless chicken breasts

6 bacon slices, cut into ¼-inch pieces

1 cup uncooked rice

1 (14½-ounce) can stewed tomatoes, undrained

1¼ cups chicken broth

2 cups packed and coarsely chopped fresh collards, mustard greens, or kale (3 to 4 ounces)

½ teaspoon seasoned salt

½ teaspoon Tabasco sauce (or more to taste)

Chopped fresh parsley (garnish)

1. In a small bowl, mix together salt, paprika, and pepper. Season both sides of each chicken breast with mixture and set aside.

2. Cook bacon in large Dutch oven over medium heat until crisp. Remove bacon and drain on paper towels. Add chicken to pan and cook 3 minutes per side until browned. Depending on size of Dutch oven, you may need to do this in batches. Remove chicken from pan when browned and set aside. Discard remaining drippings except for one tablespoon.

3. Add rice to pan and stir, cooking for 1 minute. Add tomatoes with juice, broth, greens, seasoned salt, Tabasco sauce, and half of the bacon. Bring to a boil over high heat. Remove from heat and lay chicken breasts on top of rice mixture.

4. Bake covered at 350° F for about 30 minutes or until chicken is cooked. Let stand 5 minutes before serving. Garnish with parsley if desired.

Chief the Thief

Charlie and I both are animal lovers—dog people, cat people, and we even have some fish too! However, dogs always hold a special place in our hearts. We both had dogs growing up, and when we got married, Charlie already had a Boston terrier named Bailey, and together we adopted a Boxer named Molly. We were a happy little family for years.

The food part of this story is connected to another dog, Chief. Charlie was on his way to an industry show one afternoon when the traffic came to a stand still. It was not quite rush hour, so he thought it might be due to the rain that was coming down so hard and fast that even the trees were looking for cover. As the cars inched along, he finally saw what was slowing things down. A big black dog with a spotted chest was walking between the cars, right down the yellow line and looking up desperately into every car window that went by. As Charlie drove past, though dressed and running late for his function, he pulled to the side of the road and whistled. Before he knew it, a flash of black fur had passed him and was in the passenger seat of his truck. The dog had two collars, but no nametag. I was still at work when Charlie called and said, "Just wanted you to know there's a dog in the garage at home."

Without knowing the dog's name, Charlie started talking to him, saying things like, "What's your name, Chief?" and because he was a big dog, "Where do you live, Big Chief?" The big old dog would look up, bang his tail on the floor, and arch his ears in a way that made him look like Sally Field in her "flying nun" outfit. From that first week forward, his name just became Big Chief or Chief and Chiefy for short. We tried to find his owners for a couple weeks, but no one ever stepped forward. By the end of the third week, he had become part of our little family, which was fine by us because we didn't really want to let him go. He was the sweetest, most gentle dog we had ever known.

What does this have to do with recipes and cooking you ask again? Well, ole Chief was gangly, bow-legged in the back, and almost always had a "who me?" look on his face—sweet and innocent, but he proved to be much more savvy than he looked!

One night we had gone downstairs to watch a movie after dinner and left our dishes and a plate with a couple of extra baked chicken breasts on the counter. We figured we would clean up after the show—a bad habit we

continue to this day. About halfway through the movie, we heard a thud upstairs. When noises like that occur, we always look around for the dogs to make sure they hadn't hurt themselves jumping down from a chair or our bed. Bailey was in my lap, and Molly was on the floor cozied up to a space heater, but Chief was nowhere to be seen. We went upstairs to find everything completely as we'd left it, with one exception—the extra chicken breasts! Chief was sitting in the kitchen looking very innocent with his flying nun ears, his tail banging against the floor, and that same "who me?" look on his face. He may not have been convicted of his crime except for the fact that his long muzzle smelled like lemon pepper chicken. That snout was his biggest asset and his greatest weakness in this little chicken caper. Somehow he had managed to lift himself up to the counter, just enough to get his long mouth to that chicken without disturbing a thing, and if it weren't for coming down just a bit too hard after that second piece, he'd have gotten away scot-free.

We laughed at that big old black dog, and we couldn't blame him, for in the words of Val McDermid from the book *Killing The Shadows*, "Society gets the criminals it deserves." As the head of our little society, I was stupid enough to leave the chicken on the counter, but Chief was smart enough to get him a piece…or two.

David Howard in his shop with a fresh batch of Mountain Manna Chicken Cookers.

The Classy Cooker

The OPN crew and I visited our friend David Howard at his shop Treasures in Earthen Vessels in Gatlinburg, Tennessee. We spent the morning making pottery and the afternoon cooking up a great one-pan dinner using his Mountain Manna Chicken Cooker.

You've heard of cooking chicken on a beer can, right? This is the same idea, but in the oven and in handmade pottery. The great thing about David's chicken cooker, aside from graduating from the old beer can to a nice piece of pottery, is that it's multipurpose. Since the liquid insert and dish are separate pieces, you can use it to serve chips and salsa, veggies and dip, or use the dish by itself for baking casseroles or desserts. No matter how you use it, you'll get compliments on the presentation as well as the food.

Orange Rosemary Chicken

MAKES 6 SERVINGS

(From our video recipe shoot with potter David Howard)

- 1 whole roasting chicken (with skin on)
- ⅔ cup orange juice
- 1 orange, sliced and halved
- Rosemary or orange infused olive oil
- 2 tablespoons dried or 1 tablespoon chopped, fresh rosemary
- ½ tablespoon poultry seasoning
- Salt and freshly ground black pepper
- 2 or 3 carrots, peeled and thickly sliced
- 4 or 5 small red potatoes, quartered
- 1 small red onion, quartered

1. Wash chicken and pat dry with a paper towel.
2. Pour orange juice into the insert of the chicken cooker, filling about ⅔ full. Put insert in the center of the chicken cooker and position chicken on top of insert.
3. Starting at the top of the chicken, place several halved orange slices in between the skin and meat on both sides of chicken. Coat chicken with a small amount of olive oil and pat rosemary evenly on chicken. Sprinkle on chicken seasoning, as well and season with salt and pepper.
4. Crumble a small piece of aluminum foil into a ball and place in the neck hole at the top of the chicken to contain the steam. Bake at 350° F for about 30 minutes, making sure oven rack is low enough so that chicken is several inches away from top burner.
5. After 30 minutes, remove cooker and add carrots, potatoes, onions, and remaining orange slices (in that order) to the pottery bowl at the base of the chicken. Season vegetables with salt and pepper. Return to the oven to continue cooking for at least another hour. Depending on the size of the chicken, cooking time may be longer. Chicken is done when a thermometer inserted into the thigh meat reads 165° F.
6. Remove foil plug and let rest for about 5 to 10 minutes before serving.

LUNCH & DINNER

Señor Hog and The Potter

If you know me, you know how much I love Gatlinburg, Tennessee, and the Great Smoky Mountains. I've gone there many times to work and to play, and I always come away with something new to love about that treasured part of the country.

About a year ago, we were there for a couple days and stayed at a bed and breakfast off Glades Road in the Arts & Crafts community. We had had a lazy morning after our first night, enjoying the hospitality and the breakfast, of course, and then decided to go walking in the Greenbrier area. When you get out on those trails, you can walk a good ways without realizing how far you've gone, and before you know it, you're hungry! By the time we got back to our room, it was dinnertime.

Being a little tired from the hike, we decided to stay close and ended up just a couple miles down the road at a place called Señor Hog's. Charlie and I like Mexican food, and with a name like that, it had to be good. We got a table on the deck where there was only one other gentleman. He was reading a book and enjoying a beer as the sun set over the ridges. Noticing our befuddlement with our umbrella, he kindly came over to offer assistance. Of course, I've never met a stranger and neither has Charlie for that matter, so we struck up the small talk, and the next thing you knew, we're all at the same table enjoying the finest Tex-Mex and beer that ole Señor Hog had to offer. Once again, food opened the door and invited in our new friend David Howard.

It turned out that David is a potter in Gatlinburg, and I highly recommend a visit to his store, Treasures In Earthen Vessels. I am now the proud owner of several of his pieces, and Charlie doesn't drink coffee from any mug other than the one he got from David! His talents are not just limited to clay though—he includes some recipes with his pie plate, bread baker, chicken cooker and Brie baker. These days we don't go to Gatlinburg without spending some time with David. Next time you are out at a restaurant, keep an eye out...food just might introduce you to your next friend.

Vegetable Lasagna

MAKES 6–8 SERVINGS

It was 5 p.m. one day, and I was still at my desk, knee deep in emails, recipes, and scripts—starving and with no idea in mind for supper. I went down to the kitchen and saw the bounty of veggies my sweet neighbor Regina had brought over. Next, the lasagna box in the pantry caught my eye, and I instantly thought of how Selita Reichart of Red Gold Tomatoes cooked regular lasagna noodles in the oven without boiling them. Vegetable lasagna was coming together. I decided to use the cheese mixture that Miss Pat uses for her lasagna. While definitely not traditional Italian, it is so creamy and good. About one hour later, we were eating dinner. One hour, one pan, one happy Nan…and a happy Charlie, too!

1 garlic clove, minced

2 cups prepared spaghetti sauce (I used tomato & basil variety)

1 (14½-ounce) can diced tomatoes, undrained

9 regular uncooked lasagna noodles

2 small zucchini, sliced lengthwise ¼-inch thick

1 small white or purple slender eggplant, sliced lengthwise ¼-inch thick

3 to 4 cups fresh baby spinach

Salt and freshly ground black pepper

2 tablespoons dried basil

2 tablespoons dried oregano

6 ounces cream cheese, slightly softened

⅓ cup sour cream

1 cup cottage cheese

Freshly grated Parmesan cheese for serving

1. In a large mixing bowl, combine garlic, spaghetti sauce, and tomatoes. Pour 1 cup tomato mixture in the bottom of a 7½ x 11¾-inch baking dish and spread out evenly. Lay 3 lasagna noodles lengthwise and side-by-side in pan on top of tomato mixture.

2. Place zucchini and eggplant slices on top of noodles, alternating and distributing evenly. Generously season veggies with salt and pepper and sprinkle on basil and oregano. Evenly spread spinach leaves on top and lay 3 more lasagna noodles on top of leaves.

3. In a small bowl, combine cream cheese, sour cream, and cottage cheese until well mixed. Spread on top of lasagna noodles. Lay remaining 3 noodles on top of cheese mixture and pour remaining tomato mixture all over the top and along the sides. Pan will be full. Cover tightly with foil and bake at 350° F for about 1 hour or until lasagna noodles are soft. Cool for about 5 minutes before serving and serve with freshly grated Parmesan on top.

Nan's Notes: *If you only have a 7 x 11-inch pan, make sure to sit the pan on a cookie sheet in the oven, in case any tomato sauce bubbles out.*

Desserts

Fruit Compote

MAKES 8–10 SERVINGS

My mom and I were going through her recipe collection and came across this one—handwritten by her on a piece of stationary from a glass company from home. A little fruit delight, perfect on the sour cream pound cake. As good as it is, though, the best part is what was written on the back of the recipe. My brother Denny, a little kid at the time, had written a note to Momma that said, "Mom, if you wake up, we walked up to Jon's house to get the other movie. Don't worry! We're walking through the backyards. Love, Denny." Priceless. I don't know whether my mother saved it for the recipe or the note.

1 can peach pie filling

1 (20-ounce) can pineapple chunks (drained)

1 (11-ounce) can mandarin oranges (drained)

3 ripe bananas, sliced

1 small bag frozen sliced strawberries

1. Combine all ingredients in a large bowl and mix well.

2. Serve in individual dessert dishes with whipped cream or serve over pound cake.

Fresh Berries with Brown Sugar Cream

MAKES DESIRED AMOUNT OF SERVINGS

A former roommate gave me this recipe years ago, and it continues to amaze people when they taste it. It's light, fresh, and super easy. You don't even need a pan—just parfait glasses or dessert dishes. The sweet brown sugar melts into the tangy sour cream for a perfect balance.

Fresh blueberries
Fresh raspberries
Sour cream
Brown sugar
Fresh mint sprig for garnish (optional)

1. Wash and drain berries. Arrange a mixture of both berries in serving glasses or dishes.

2. Place a generous dollop of sour cream on the top and sprinkle brown sugar on the sour cream. Serve immediately.

Nan's Notes: *There really are no measurements—put as much of each ingredient as you want. Try different amounts of everything until you find the balance that you like.*

DESSERTS

Grapes and Good Friends

When I was Miss Mississippi many moons ago, a wonderful lady from Vicksburg, Mississippi, named Jennie Akers was my traveling companion/chaperone. You know us young southern girls absolutely must have a chaperone! I first met Jennie when she was lead hostess of the group of ladies that took care of the contestants during pageant week.

When I became Miss Mississippi, I was somewhat of an ambassador for the state, and Jennie and I toured through all the counties in sponsored Cadillacs and Continentals. I would speak and perform at civic functions, grand openings, ride in parades, etc. Jennie was so proud of me that she made me carry a "boom box" in the car, and whenever there was an opportunity to sing, she'd find an outlet, plug it in, and pop in my cassette tape of tracks to Jeffery Osborne's "On The Wings of Love" or Barbara Streisand's "Woman In The Moon". I might be singing for 100 people in a park or 2 people at a gas station. It didn't matter to Jennie because whether the people were having a picnic or buying gas, she saw it as an opportunity for me to represent the state and do my job as such representative. She was always there for me and had my back, too.

Once, she even tried to talk me out of getting a speeding ticket. "Awffisuh," she said, "Do you re-uh-lyze this is Miss Missuhssippi?" she said in her authentic Southern drawl. But I had a less-than-impressed officer that day who simply responded, "Yes ma'am, I see that by the sign on the car door, ma'am, and do you know what happens if you and Miss Mississippi hit a deer at 80 miles per hour?" Needless to say, this was one instance where two southern belles and all their charm just couldn't talk their way out of something.

Jennie was the perfect travel mate for me too, because she would always bring things to eat with her. When you're on the road, it's good to have someone with you who carries snacks. I'd feel the need for a bite of something, and she'd start digging around in her purse. No matter what she actually had in there, she'd always say, "Ah,ve gaught uh Tootsie Roll, uh candy bar, and ah think ah've got a grape in he'uh too."

Creamy Grape Parfait

MAKES 4 SERVINGS

1½ pounds grapes (combination of red and green)

4 ounces cream cheese, softened

4 ounces sour cream

¼ teaspoon vanilla extract

2 tablespoons sugar

1 cup chopped pecans

½ cup brown sugar

Nan's Notes: *The grape mixture keeps in the fridge for several days so you can make it up ahead of time—just don't put the topping on until ready to serve.*

1. Remove grapes from stems, rinse, and drain well. To remove any remaining water, lay grapes on a dishtowel and pat dry.

2. In a large mixing bowl, cream the cream cheese, sour cream, vanilla, and sugar. Gently fold in grapes, making sure to thoroughly coat. Cover bowl and refrigerate overnight.

3. When ready to serve, place chopped pecans and brown sugar in a large nonstick skillet over medium heat. Stir constantly for about 3 to 5 minutes only, allowing pecans to brown a bit and brown sugar to harden and crisp up. Remove from heat and put into a bowl to cool for a few minutes.

4. In individual parfait or dessert glasses, sprinkle pecan mixture on bottom, followed by a serving of grape mixture, and finish with the pecan mixture sprinkled on top. If serving in parfait glasses, add more layers, ending with pecans on top. Serve immediately.

Charlie's Chocolate Bread Pudding

MAKES 8 SERVINGS

This is not your every day dessert, but if you're going to be a bear, be a grizzly. This one is definitely big, bold, and if you're on a diet... dangerous.

2 cups heavy cream

⅓ cup sugar

¼ cup milk

6 ounces semisweet chocolate chips

2 large eggs, room temperature

1 teaspoon vanilla extract

¾ teaspoon orange extract

6 ounces day-old French bread, cut into ¾-inch cubes (about 4 cups)

Whipped cream

1. In a medium saucepan, heat cream, sugar, and milk over medium heat until sugar dissolves, stirring occasionally. Remove from heat.

2. Add chocolate chips and stir until mixture is smooth and chocolate melts completely. Cool for a few minutes.

3. Beat eggs in a large bowl. When chocolate mixture has cooled a bit, slowly whisk in mixture to the egg bowl, a little at a time and blend well. Add in vanilla and orange extracts and stir.

4. Place bread in a shallow 8 x 8-inch glass or ceramic baking dish and pour chocolate mixture over bread. Cover and refrigerate 30 minutes, stirring occasionally.

5. Bake uncovered at 300° F for 40 to 45 minutes or until set. Cool 10 minutes and serve warm or cover and refrigerate to serve later. Serve with whipped cream.

Cindy Black serving up the best bread pudding I've ever had!

Discovering Dessert

You never have to ask me twice to travel to Gatlinburg, Tennessee, especially when I make a new friend AND discover one of my all-time favorite desserts, **Amaretto Bread Pudding**. I met Cindy Black through Marci Claude, another Gatlinburg friend, and we immediately hit it off. We already had the food thing in common, and like me, she loves to snow ski and go to New York to see Broadway shows! Cindy worked for many years at the well-known The Wild Plum Tea Room in Gatlinburg. This recipe comes courtesy of them and has been loved by many customers there throughout the years.

Cindy is now Assistant Director of the Smoky Mountain Area Rescue Ministries, and she's got a heart of gold, in addition to expertise in the kitchen. I've never had anything like this bread pudding—it is that good!

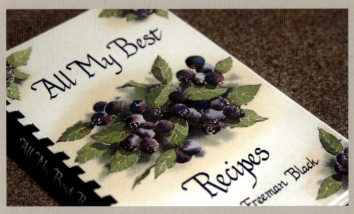

I'm proud to have a copy of Cindy's cookbook in my own collection.

Amaretto Bread Pudding

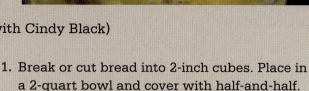

MAKES 12 SERVINGS

(From our video recipe shoot with Cindy Black)

1 loaf French bread
1 quart half-and-half
2 tablespoons butter, room temperature
3 eggs
1½ cups sugar
2 tablespoons almond extract
¾ cup golden raisins
¾ cup sliced almonds
Whipped cream (for topping)

AMARETTO SAUCE:
8 tablespoons butter, room temperature
1 cup powdered sugar
1 egg, well beaten
4 tablespoons amaretto liqueur

1. Break or cut bread into 2-inch cubes. Place in a 2-quart bowl and cover with half-and-half. Cover bowl and let stand 1 hour.

2. Preheat oven to 325° F. Grease a 9 x 13-inch baking dish with butter.

3. In a small bowl, beat eggs, sugar, and almond extract. Stir into bread mixture. Gently fold in raisins and almonds. Spread in baking dish and bake 50 minutes or until golden brown and pudding is set.

4. In top of a double boiler, place butter and powdered sugar. Stir until dissolved and very hot. Remove from heat and cool for a few minutes.

5. Whisk in a couple of tablespoons of warm butter mixture to the beaten egg. Stir well. Add another couple of tablespoons to bring egg temperature up and whisk well. Pour beaten egg with additional tablespoons into double boiler with remaining butter/sugar mixture and stir. Add amaretto and blend.

6. Serve bread pudding warm with warm amaretto sauce and whipped cream.

Cheesecake Cup with Cookie Crumble

MAKES 6 SERVINGS

Like Charlie and me, our friends the Hendricks' are a Yankee/Southerner couple. Lee is from West Virginia, and Molly is from Minnesota. When we get together, we always laugh at each other's north/south differences, but one thing we all agree on is good food! Lee was grilling up some special steaks one night, and we were invited to dinner. I was put in charge of the dessert. I had already gotten a great pretzel turtles recipe from Molly for my first book, so I knew I had to bring something good and this is what I brought.

Molly likes Biscoff cookies, and they are the perfect complement to this refreshing spin on traditional cheesecake. This is something you can whip up quickly, too. The fresh lime juice and zest balances out the richness of the cheesecake. It turned out to be a hit on both sides of our marital Mason-Dixon line!

- 2 cups fresh strawberries, cored and sliced
- 2 tablespoons sugar
- 1 package no bake cheesecake mix
- 1 teaspoon lime zest
- 1 tablespoon Key lime juice
- 6 crunchy gourmet cookies, crumbled (I used Biscoff)
- Several extra whole cookies and lime slices (for garnish)

1. Stir strawberries and 2 tablespoons sugar together in a small bowl and refrigerate.

2. In a medium bowl, mix up no bake cheesecake according to directions on package. Add lime zest and lime juice and stir to combine. Chill for 30 minutes or more.

3. Sprinkle some crumbled cookies in the bottoms of 6 dessert dishes or ramekins and place a few strawberries on top. Spoon cheesecake mixture into each and sprinkle with remaining crumbled cookies. Top with remaining strawberries and garnish each dish with a ½ cookie and a lime slice. Serve immediately.

Nan's Notes: *You could also substitute blueberries for the strawberries or add both.*

Raspberry Chocolate Tarts

MAKES 6 SERVINGS

Sometimes I buy shoes and come up with an outfit to wear with them after the fact. That's the same principle for how this recipe came to be. I saw these adorable tart pans at Williams-Sonoma and figured I needed them. Tart pans need tarts, and while raspberries don't necessarily need chocolate, they sure taste great together.

- 1 refrigerated pie crust for a 9-inch pie
- 2 teaspoons cornstarch
- 6 tablespoons sugar
- 2 (6-ounce) containers fresh raspberries, washed and drained
- ¼ cup slice almonds
- ¼ to ½ cup chocolate chips (milk or dark chocolate)

CRUMBLE:
- ½ cup flour
- ¼ cup sugar
- 2 tablespoons brown sugar
- ½ teaspoon almond extract
- 2 tablespoons butter, chilled and cubed

Nan's Notes: *This recipe is for six 4-inch individual tart pans. Tender, flakey pie dough works great for these little tarts, but if you modify this recipe for a 9-inch tart pan, you'll probably want to use traditional tart dough that is firmer and more crumbly.*

1. Prepare crust per package instructions. Roll crust out onto a flat surface and divide into 6 pieces, with each piece being a couple of inches larger in diameter than each 4-inch tart pan.

2. Place a piece of dough in each pan, pressing down along the bottom and sides. Tear off any excess. Refrigerate for 15 minutes.

3. After chilling, pierce each crust several times with a fork and bake according to package directions, being careful not to get too brown. Set tarts pans aside and cool completely.

4. Mix together cornstarch and sugar in a medium bowl. Add raspberries and toss gently. Sprinkle with almonds and mix gently.

5. In a small mixing bowl, place flour, sugar, brown sugar, almond extract, and butter. Mix together well with a pastry cutter or with your hands until the mixture is crumbly.

6. Sprinkle enough chocolate chips in each tart pan to cover the bottom. Spoon in the raspberry mixture evenly on top of the chips. Sprinkle the crumble evenly on top.

7. Bake at 375° F for about 30 minutes or until the top is golden brown and the fruit is bubbly hot. Serve warm with ice cream or at room temperature with whipped cream and fresh raspberries on top.

July 4th Berry Tart

MAKES 10–12 SERVINGS

I've made this little tart for so many 4th of Julys, but you don't have to wait for Independence Day to enjoy it. Flag Day, Veterans Day, and Memorial Day—all fitting to me. It's pretty, festive, and a tasty addition to your celebratory picnics and family gatherings, and in the heat of the summer, it's a light dessert that won't weigh you down.

1 refrigerated pie crust, room temperature

1 (8-ounce) package cream cheese, softened

1 (8-ounce) container sour cream

¼ cup sugar

Fresh strawberries, cored and thickly sliced

Fresh blueberries

1 (13-ounce) can sweetened whipped cream

1. On a large baking sheet (with no sides), shape pie crust into a rectangle and bake according to directions on the package. Cool thoroughly on baking sheet.

2. In a small bowl, mix together cream cheese, sour cream, and sugar. Spread filling evenly on cooled, baked crust.

3. Layer fruit in the American flag design, alternating strawberry slices with whipped cream for the stripes, and for the stars, fill in the area with blueberries and dot whipped cream throughout. Chill and serve.

Nan's Notes: *Use a baking sheet with no sides so that you can easily slide the tart onto your serving piece.*

Red Wine Strawberry Sauce

MAKES 4 SERVINGS

I can't tell you how many times I have served these two sauces! These are so easy to make, and they make a great impression. The banana one is my go-to wintertime homerun for dessert, and strawberry is perfect for fresh summertime berries. Courtesy of my former roomie, Miss Karen.

2 pints strawberries

¼ cup red wine

3 tablespoons sugar

1 cinnamon stick, 3-inches long

Dash of ground black pepper

Sliced pound cake (recipe on page 191) or vanilla ice cream for serving

Whipped cream for topping

1. Core and slice strawberries and set aside.

2. In a large skillet over medium-high heat, cook wine, sugar, and cinnamon stick until sugar dissolves. Add strawberries and dash of black pepper and simmer for about 3 or 4 minutes.

3. Remove the cinnamon stick and serve sauce over sliced pound cake or ice cream. Top with whipped cream.

Brown Sugar Banana Sauce

MAKES 4 SERVINGS

2 bananas

¼ cup white wine

3 tablespoons brown sugar

1 teaspoon cinnamon

Vanilla ice cream for serving

Pirouline rolled wafers for serving (optional)

1. Slice bananas and set aside.

2. Combine white wine, sugar, and cinnamon in a large skillet. Cook over medium-high heat until sugar dissolves, about 3 minutes. Add bananas and cook until bananas soften slightly, about 3 or 4 minutes.

3. Remove from heat and serve over vanilla ice cream in dessert dishes with a wafer, if desired.

Grace Ann's Peach Cobbler

MAKES 8–10 SERVINGS

2 (8-ounce) cans crescent rolls

1 (8-ounce) package cream cheese, softened

¾ cup sugar

½ stick butter, melted

1 (21-ounce) can peach pie filling

1 (8¼-ounce) can peaches, drained

GLAZE:

1 cup powdered sugar

2 tablespoons milk

1. Preheat oven to 375° F. In a 9 x 13-inch baking dish, roll out one package of rolls in bottom of pan, sealing perforations.

2. In a small bowl, cream sugar with cream cheese and spread over rolls. Combine pie filling and peaches in a small bowl and stir to blend. Spread peach combination over cream cheese mixture.

3. Roll out remaining can of rolls, sealing perforations, and place on top. Pour melted butter evenly over pan. Bake for 20 to 25 minutes or until brown.

4. In a small bowl, mix together powdered sugar and milk. Pour on top of cobbler. Serve warm with vanilla ice cream.

Paging Miss Nashville

When I was growing up, we went to church with a wonderful cook, Grace Ann Carter, and we often went by her house after the service to eat with her and her family. Grace Ann and her sister Carolyn Mitchell were very special to us. Momma did their hair for many years, and Carolyn and her husband J. Hugh were like parents to me and helped move me to Nashville when I got hired at Opryland. Carolyn always called me "Miss Nashville"—even paging me in a store one time as such, while I was home in Hattiesburg. I was digging through the bargain bin at Hudson's Salvage, as I had done many times before, when it came over the loudspeaker. I didn't catch it at first because of the assortment of fire sale items I had my hands on, but then it hit me. I stopped and looked up across the store, and there was Carolyn, waving and grinning. I miss Grace Ann, Momma Carolyn and Papa J. Hugh. I don't think Grace Ann would mind that I added more peaches to this recipe because one can never have too many peaches in a peach cobbler.

Teamwork— On the Job & In the Kitchen

The firefighters at Station 29 here in Nashville love their jobs and the camaraderie that comes with it. I imagine that's true for all firefighters around our country. It takes teamwork, hustle, and attention, or someone might get hurt or worse. Therefore, these folks deserve a treat every now and then, and Firefighter Chris Tomlinson (aka Pooh) showed me how to make an easy, delicious dessert during our shoot at Station 29.

Everybody at the fire hall loves this **Firehouse Cobbler**, and the One Pan Nan crew and I became fans of it real quick, too! Treat yourself and your family to this one, and maybe even drop one by your local fire station to say thanks. They'll appreciate it, I guarantee.

Firehouse Cobbler

MAKES 10–12 SERVINGS

(From our video recipe shoot at Station 29/Nashville Fire Department)

- 1 stick butter
- 2 cups flour
- 2 cups buttermilk
- 2 cups sugar
- 1 (21-ounce) can fruit pie filling (your choice)
- Cinnamon (for sprinkling on top)

1. Preheat oven to 350° F. Melt butter in a large cast iron skillet or baking pan in oven.

2. In a large bowl, mix together flour, buttermilk, and sugar. Remove pan of melted butter from oven and pour flour mixture into pan (do not stir). Pour fruit evenly over the mixture (do not stir) and sprinkle cinnamon on top. Bake for 45 minutes or until done. Serve warm with vanilla ice cream.

No firefighter is in jeopardy of losing his or her job to me. It's a good thing Engineer Tracy Townsend had my back.

Perms, Pies & People I Love

The movie *Steel Magnolias* could just as easily have been set in Hattiesburg, Mississippi, as it was in Natchitoches, Louisiana, and my mother could have played Dolly Parton's character, Truvy. Momma has been a hairdresser for over 50 years, and some of the scenes from that movie seem like they were taken straight from some of the beauty shops where she's worked. Her longest stretch with clippers and scissors was at Head Hunters, as the owner for many years and then staying on after she sold the business to her friend, Libbie Lott—affectionately known as "Boss Lady." Momma has also curled up and dyed at Kitty's, Belle & Beau, and now with the gals at Backstage & Company in Hattiesburg.

Feeling right at home

What does that have to do with food? All of my momma's clients love her because she loves them. She always tries to accommodate their schedules and take care of them, sometimes in ways that go beyond a beautiful updo. They do the same for her. They do what southern women do—they bring gifts of food…lots of it. Momma has the lock on the best food in Hattiesburg because it gets delivered to the beauty shop, especially when her ladies know her kids are coming home. Their signature dishes have been a part of every one of our family gatherings: Georgia Bryant's Chocolate Dessert, Carmen Simmons' Pecan Pie, Gay Hanberry's Date Nut Bars, Gay Nell Wallace's Christmas Candy, Jo Newman's Sausage Casserole, Mary Henderson's Chocolate Chip Cake, Alice Bivens' Strawberry Bread, Doris Rouse's Breakfast Casserole, and Anne Jones' Sugar Cookies & Pound Cake. Whew, try saying all that in one breath! I am sure I'm forgetting a few—there were so many delicious treats.

Knowing that any one of these scrumptious snacks might be at the shop on any given day, I'd go there after school to sweep the floors, clean the combs, pull the paper off the perm rods, and cross my fingers for a tasty reward for a job well done. It was a social event as much as it was to help Momma. All us gals gabbing while momma blow-dried and backcombed. She was good at it, and her ladies loved her for it. Like Truvy and I always say, the higher the hair, the closer you are to God. Can I get an amen, please!

I loved being in the shop, I loved those ladies, and whenever I got a hankering for some date nut bars, I'd say, "Momma, let's call Gay and see if she needs to get her hair done."

Kelley Family Chocolate Pie

MAKES 8 SERVINGS

My husband Charlie pines for chocolate more than he does for me. He gets it honest. If there was no other chocolate choice in the house, his daddy would tip back the bottle of chocolate syrup from the fridge just to get his chocolate fix...on a daily basis! Yes, their blood runs milk chocolate brown.

The first time I had this pie, it all made sense. This is the best chocolate pie I've ever eaten, period. No holiday meal in the Kelley house is complete without this pie at the end. Top it with real whipped cream, and you'll sate even the most discerning of chocoholics!

3 tablespoons butter

1 cup sugar

¼ cup flour

1 egg, room temperature

¼ cup milk

2 ounces unsweetened chocolate squares

Pinch of salt

1 teaspoon vanilla extract

1 baked pie shell (in an 8-inch pie plate)

Whipped cream (for serving)

1. Place 2 to 3 inches water in the bottom of a double boiler. Heat on high until water is boiling.

2. Lower the heat to medium and position the top pan over water. Put butter, sugar, and flour in the top pan and cook until butter has melted. Stir to incorporate well. Mixture will be crumbly.

3. Beat egg and milk together in a small bowl and pour into mixture. Mix thoroughly until smooth.

4. Add in chocolate, stirring occasionally as chocolate melts. Cook until mixture is thick and pudding-like in consistency. Add a pinch of salt and gently blend.

5. Remove from heat and separate double boiler, allowing pie filling to cool for about 10 minutes. Pour in vanilla extract and stir gently to mix.

6. Pour into baked pie shell and chill. Serve with whipped cream.

Nan's Notes: *Miss Pat always uses an 8-inch pie plate, but a 9-inch is fine, as well—pie will just not be as thick.*

Orange Frisco Cake

MAKES 1 (9-INCH) LOAF

I made this cake for the birthday of a man who is like a father to me, Cliff Ward. Cliff grew up in San Francisco, so this cake is a hometown tip of the hat to the city's much-loved native son. If you like orange flavor, no matter if you've been to San Francisco or not, you'll love this cake!

¼ cup shortening

¾ cup sugar

2 eggs, separated

4½ tablespoons orange marmalade

1 tablespoon grated orange rind

2 tablespoons chopped orange peel

½ cup chopped walnuts

2 cups flour

1 teaspoon salt

2 teaspoons baking powder

⅓ cup water

GLAZE:

½ cup powdered sugar

1 to 2 tablespoons milk

⅛ teaspoon orange extract

Nan's Notes: *Check for doneness prior to 45 minutes, depending on your oven and the color of your loaf pan. A darker pan may cook faster. I turn the cake halfway through. Serve with ice cream for dessert or as a coffee cake for breakfast or brunch.*

1. In a large bowl, cream together sugar and shortening until light and fluffy. Add egg yolks, orange marmalade, grated rind, chopped peel, and walnuts.

2. Sift flour, salt, and baking powder together in a small bowl. Add flour mixture gradually to egg and orange bowl, followed by a portion of the water, and mix well. Repeat until all flour and water is incorporated.

3. Beat egg whites until stiff and fold into batter. Pour batter into a well-greased loaf pan and bake at 350° F for about 45 to 50 minutes or until done. Sides should be brown and pulled away from pan when done. Check at 45 minutes by inserting knife into the center. If knife comes out clean, the cake is done. If it doesn't, bake a couple of minutes more and check again. Don't over bake.

4. Immediately remove cake from pan by flipping cake over on a plate, position to right side up, and cool for a few minutes before glazing.

5. Mix sugar, milk, and extract together in a small bowl, adding milk to desired consistency and drizzle on top of entire cake. May also drizzle each piece individually prior to serving.

Nannie Broome's Sour Cream Pound Cake

MAKES 12–14 SERVINGS

Just reading this recipe written in my nannie's handwriting is very special to me…let alone making it. If my mom and nannie both could be here, we could sit down with some cake and coffee and figure out a few of life's problems. I hope this cake brings you as much joy as it has our family for years.

- 3 cups sugar
- 2 sticks butter, softened
- 6 eggs, room temperature
- 1 cup sour cream
- 3 cups flour

1. In a large mixing bowl, cream sugar and butter together with a mixer until light and fluffy.

2. Add in eggs one at a time and mix well. Add in sour cream and gradually stir in flour. Mix well and pour into a greased and lightly floured tube pan. Bake at 350° F for 1 hour or until a long wooden toothpick or skewer inserted down into the cake comes out clean.

Nan's Notes: *Several desserts like pecan pie or banana pudding probably come to mind as the quintessential Southern dessert, but I'll throw in a nomination for the pound cake. You can do so much with it. It's the little black dress of desserts—serve it plain, with strawberry or chocolate sauce, or fresh fruit and whipped cream on top.*

Nan's Notes: *You can find limoncello at any liquor store if you don't make it yourself or have a handy neighbor like I do.*

Limoncello Pound Cake

MAKES 1 (9-INCH) LOAF

If you've ever been to Italy and sampled some of the local drink, then you know about limoncello. Made of lemon peel, sugar, and spirits, I actually had my first taste of it in Slovenia, Italy's neighbor. My next encounter with limoncello was with my herb-growing, gardening-inspiration neighbor, Regina. She makes it herself and has been sharing her bounty with me for a couple years now. My other neighbor Holley used Regina's limoncello to make this yummy and potent pound cake. Holley shared the recipe with me, and if I could speak Italian, I would espouse the taste of this lovely, lemony cake with an accent like Pavarotti's.

1 box lemon cake mix

1 (3¼-ounce) box lemon instant pudding/pie filling

3 eggs

⅓ cup oil

1 cup limoncello

GLAZE:

½ cup powdered sugar

1 to 2 tablespoons limoncello

1. In a large bowl, mix all the ingredients together with a hand mixer. Pour into a well-greased loaf pan and bake at 350° F for 55 to 60 minutes. Cake is done when a toothpick inserted into the center comes out clean. Allow cake to cool a bit.

2. Mix glaze ingredients in a small bowl to the desired consistency. Drizzle over entire cake and drizzle each piece when serving. Serve with vanilla ice cream.

Slow Cooker Cake

MAKES 10–12 SERVINGS

Yes, Virginia there is a Santa Claus, and you can bake a cake in a slow cooker. This cake is so moist and delicious. Once you get it all going in the slow cooker, you walk away and return later to a scrumptious dessert. One night, I used our dinner guests as guinea pigs and tried this recipe out on them. I do this every now and then, and it makes Charlie so nervous that he keeps a stash of Pepperidge Farms cookies hidden in his studio… just in case!

Thankfully, this was a home run and continues to be a favorite, fudgy phenomenon. Leave a piece of this out for Santa this year instead of cookies, and he might leave you an extra present.

- 2 eggs
- 1 cup milk
- ½ cup vegetable oil
- 1½ teaspoons vanilla extract
- 2 cups sugar
- 1¾ cups flour
- ¾ cup unsweetened cocoa powder
- 1½ teaspoons baking soda
- 1½ teaspoons baking powder
- ½ teaspoon salt

1. Spray slow cooker pan with cooking spray. In a medium bowl, whisk together eggs, milk, oil, and vanilla until well mixed.

2. Whisk in 1 cup boiling water, followed by the remaining dry ingredients. Mix thoroughly. Pour the cake batter into the slow cooker pan. Lay a dishtowel across the top of the slow cooker, making sure the sides do not come in contact with the hot plate.

3. Place lid on top and set control to low. Cook for 3 hours or until the sides of the cake have pulled away from the pan and the top of the cake has no apparent spots that look wet. Once done, turn slow cooker off and let cake sit for about 30 minutes. Serve warm with vanilla ice cream.

Nan's Notes: *The dishtowel helps absorb some of the condensation that collects on the inside of the lid and keeps it from dripping down on the cake. A tip for the slow cooker that applies to grilling, too—if you're looking, it's not cooking! Don't be tempted to lift the lid and look, or you'll need to cook it a little longer.*

The Tale of the Brown Wedding Cake

When you think of wedding cakes, you probably have visions of multi-tiered, white-iced, exquisitely decorated towers of deliciousness. Who doesn't like wedding cakes? Charlie loves them, and he told me his mother would usually bring home a small piece of reception heaven from every wedding she went to. When we decided to get married, we struggled with when, where, and who to invite, as all young couples do. However, for me there was never a question about the cake.

Since we were young and broke back then, the "when" to get married became July when Charlie's family had a vacation already planned. The "where" became the Outer Banks of North Carolina because that's where the vacation was taking place, and the "who to invite" became just our immediate families since half of the guests would already be at the beach. The cake needed to come from Mississippi because that's where the one I wanted was made, by Yvonne Owens, a family friend for years.

So, Yvonne made it, and my mother drove it—from Hattiesburg, Mississippi, across Alabama, through parts of Georgia, and finally to arrive safely on the coast of Carolina. My Baptist family and his Catholic family gathered on the beach to watch us get married by a Methodist minister dressed in shorts and a Hawaiian shirt. We had dinner afterwards at a local seafood restaurant, and then headed back to the beach house for the grand finale, the cake.

I know Charlie was dreaming of that big white wedding cake decorated with ribbons of white icing and pastel flowers, but when he opened the box, he saw a light brown cake about the color of a camel hair coat, trimmed with brown-icing roses. However, this was no ordinary brown cake. This was Yvonne's famous caramel cake, and my favorite of all time! It was what I grew up on, and it is one of the finest cakes I have ever eaten. So, when Momma asked me what she could bring, Yvonne's caramel cake was the first thing I thought of. A traditional wedding cake never crossed my mind. Now ole Charlie may not have known what to think when he saw it, but when he tasted it, his sweet tooth knew it had hit the confectionery lottery.

Even though he still jokes about it, there's no denying that our caramel wedding cake came through and delivered what a wedding cake is supposed to—good luck to the couple. After all, we have been married 14 years now, and I'll take that over a big, fancy, white cake any day.

DESSERTS 197

Banana Split Cake

MAKES 8–10 SERVINGS

Who doesn't love a classic banana split from the ice cream parlor? This has all of those elements—bananas, pineapple, cherries, nuts, and whipped topping, just no ice cream. I can't believe I'm saying this, because ice cream is my weakness, but I didn't miss it! Full of fruity sweetness, but not heavy at all. Perfect for the summertime sweet tooth.

- 2 cups graham cracker crumbs (or crushed waffle cones, see notes)
- 6 tablespoons butter, melted
- 2 egg whites, room temperature
- 1 cup powdered sugar
- 1 stick butter, room temperature
- 4 or 5 bananas
- 1 (20-ounce) can crushed pineapple, drained well
- 1 (8-ounce) container whipped topping
- 1 (12-ounce) jar maraschino cherries, chopped (I use jumbo size)
- 1 cup chopped pecans

1. Sprinkle graham cracker crumbs or waffle cone crumbs evenly in a 7½ x 11-inch pan and pour melted butter on top. Using a fork, blend well, and with your hands, press crumbs firmly into the bottom of pan to form a crust. Refrigerate for at least 30 minutes to set up.

2. In the last 10 minutes of crust setting up, add egg whites, powdered sugar, and butter to a mixing bowl. Beat with a mixer on high for at least 10 minutes until very creamy. Spread filling on top of the crust.

3. Slice bananas and lay on top of the filling, overlapping if needed. Sprinkle crushed pineapple on top of bananas. Spread whipped topping evenly on top of the pineapple, and return to fridge. Sprinkle with cherries and pecans right before serving.

Nan's Notes: *Make sure to mix the filling for at least 10 minutes on high with a mixer, scrapping sides of the bowl along the way. If preparing the waffle cone crust, grind 12 cones (you can buy them in a package of 12) in a food processor to a rough flour consistency.*

German Apple Cake

MAKES 8–10 SERVINGS

My mom had this recipe in her collection, handwritten on a piece of paper, and begging for me to give it a try. It's fried apple pie meets apple cobbler, posing as a chewy cake. Perfect for the fall season and a dessert that keeps for several days.

- 2 large eggs
- 1 cup vegetable oil
- 2 cups sugar
- 1 teaspoon baking soda
- 2 cups flour
- 2 teaspoons cinnamon
- 1 cup chopped nuts
- 4 cups peeled, chopped apples

1. In a large mixing bowl, beat eggs and oil until foamy. Add in sugar and mix.

2. In a small bowl, dissolve baking soda into 1½ teaspoons water and pour into batter. Add flour and cinnamon and mix well. Batter will be thick.

3. Fold in nuts and apples until well incorporated. Spread batter into a greased 9 x 13-inch pan. Bake at 350° F for 50 to 60 minutes. Cool completely before serving.

Nan's Notes: *You can make this up a day ahead, pop the individual servings into the microwave for a few seconds, and serve with vanilla ice cream—delicious and addictive.*

Spiced Ginger Cookies

MAKES APPROXIMATELY 3 DOZEN

This was one of Charlie's favorite cookies growing up. Cinnamon, cloves, ginger, and chewy in the middle. I get a taste for these in the fall and winter when I'm burning those lovely spiced-scented candles, but sugar and spice is welcomed all year round.

¾ cup shortening

1 cup sugar

¼ cup molasses

1 egg, slightly beaten

2 cups flour

2 teaspoons baking soda

1 teaspoon cinnamon

1 teaspoon ground cloves

1 teaspoon ground ginger

Sugar (for coating)

1. In a large bowl, cream shortening and sugar with a mixer. Add in molasses and egg and mix well. Sift together flour, baking soda, and spices and add to mixture. Blend well.

2. Cover dough and chill in the refrigerator for at least 1 hour. Roll dough into balls about 1-inch each in diameter. Roll balls in sugar to coat completely. Place on greased baking sheet and bake at 350° F for 10 minutes.

3. Cool for 3 to 4 minutes on baking sheet, then transfer to racks to cool completely.

Nan's Notes: *These will appear puffed upon removal from the oven, but when they cool, they'll drop and get that classic cracked surface. You could serve these with the Creamy Pumpkin Dip (recipe on page 22).*

Seven Layer Bars

MAKES 10–12 SERVINGS

If you have a sweet tooth, this will satisfy it—I promise. Very rich and decadent and very little effort to make. Miss Pat's been making these for years.

- ½ cup butter
- 1 cup graham cracker crumbs
- 1 (6-ounce) package chocolate chips
- 1 (6-ounce) package butterscotch chips
- 1⅓ cups flaked coconut
- ½ cup chopped pecans
- 1 (14-ounce) can sweetened condensed milk

1. Preheat oven to 350° F. Melt butter in a 9 x 13-inch pan in the oven.
2. Sprinkle graham cracker crumbs evenly over butter. Layer with chocolate and butterscotch pieces, coconut, and pecans. Pour milk over all. Bake at 350° F for 30 minutes. Cool and cut into squares to serve.

Nan's Notes: You just might have everything in your pantry right now to whip this up for dessert. They freeze well, too. For easy crumbs in no time, put graham crackers in a plastic storage bag, squeeze out excess air, seal, and crush crackers with a rolling pin.

Cornmeal Cookies

MAKES 50–60 COOKIES

I had not heard of cornmeal cookies before, but this recipe is another newly discovered gem I found in my nannie's recipe collection. They're not overly sweet, and they have a nice cornmeal crunch to them. I added the glaze, and I think it gives them a perfect finish. If you're a fan of shortbread cookies, give these a try.

- 1 cup shortening
- 1½ cups sugar
- 2 eggs
- 1 teaspoon lemon extract
- 3 cups sifted flour
- 1 teaspoon baking powder
- ½ teaspoon salt
- 1 teaspoon nutmeg
- 1 cup cornmeal
- ½ cup raisins

GLAZE:

- ½ to 1 cup powdered sugar
- 1 to 2 tablespoons real lemon juice

1. In a large mixing bowl, cream shortening and gradually add in sugar until well incorporated and creamy. Beat in eggs until light and fluffy.

2. Add lemon extract and blend. Sift together flour, baking powder, salt, nutmeg, and cornmeal. Add to creamed mixture, mixing thoroughly.

3. Add raisins and blend. Dough will be crumbly. Blend with hands to form into workable dough and flatten on a floured surface with a roller to about ⅛-inch thick. May cut out cookies with a cookie cutter or roll dough into quarter-sized balls. Place balls of dough on greased baking sheet and press each one flat with a fork to the noted thickness.

4. Bake at 400° F for 6 to 8 minutes. Do not over bake—cookies should be just golden brown on the bottom. Cool on wire racks.

5. While cookies are cooling, mix sugar and lemon juice together in a small bowl. Adjust amounts for both, depending on desired consistency. When cookies are cooled, drizzle glaze on top of each.

DESSERTS

Spiced Tea Cookies

MAKES ABOUT 42–46 COOKIES

For Charlie, it's all about a cookie. He grew up more on cookies and cakes, and I grew up more on pies and cakes. We both love this one. Part cookie, part shortbread, and part biscuit. It's perfect for afternoon tea or coffee, and it meets all of my one-pan criteria, too.

4 chai tea bags

2 cups flour

1 cup sugar

¼ teaspoon salt

1 teaspoon ground cinnamon

1 teaspoon ground cardamom

¼ teaspoon ground ginger

¼ teaspoon ground cloves

½ teaspoon vanilla extract

½ teaspoon almond extract

1 cup butter, sliced into pats

Nan's Notes: *If you have any chai tea drinkers in your house, then you've got the tea on hand, and the rest of the ingredients are staples. You can also make up the dough ahead of time, and keep it in the freezer until you're ready to bake.*

1. Cut open tea bags and pour tea into the bowl of a food processor. Pulse for a few seconds to pulverize tea.

2. Sift together flour, sugar, and salt in a large mixing bowl. Add in cinnamon, cardamom, ground ginger, ground cloves, tea from bags, and blend well.

3. Add vanilla and almond extracts and cut in butter using a pastry blender until butter is broken down into small crumbles. Using hands, shape into dough. Work dough to blend all together and divide dough into 2 pieces.

4. Shape each piece into a log about 8 or 9 inches long. Wrap each log in wax paper and roll on the countertop to smooth out as though you're rolling a rolling pin.

5. Freeze dough in wax paper for at least 30 minutes or longer and remove when ready to bake.

6. Preheat oven to 375° F. With a sharp knife, slice chilled/frozen dough into ⅓-inch slices. Place on an ungreased baking sheet and bake for about 10 to 12 minutes or until the edges turn golden brown. Cool for about 5 minutes and then transfer to wire racks to finish cooling.

Me and Miss Pat—I couldn't ask for a better mother-in-law!

Family Treasures

I like to think my mother-in-law and I are somewhat kindred spirits—we'll both get tickled at something and laugh until we cry, and we both welcome any and all chances to sit down and enjoy a cup of coffee and a donut.

Years ago at the beginning of my cooking adventure, Miss Pat always supported, encouraged, and ate my efforts in the kitchen, even when I tried to serve her a not-quite-done turkey at the first Thanksgiving Charlie and I hosted after we started dating. Lesson learned on baking turkeys—make sure the bird is totally thawed before you put it in the oven because if his little tail is frozen shut then: a) it probably needs a little more time to thaw, and b) you haven't removed the bag of frozen "parts" that needs to be removed before cooking. Thankfully, Miss Pat figured out why the bird wasn't getting done without passing judgment on my turkey ignorance. Though dinner was late that year, we were together, and we still have a great laugh years later about the turkey with the frozen tail! Since that fateful Thanksgiving, she has always offered to let me in on all of the Kelley family's favorite recipes and skillfully steered me away from some pitfalls of beginner cooks.

No telling how many batches of **Christmas Sugar Cookies** (recipe on next page) she's made through the years. When she brings us a plate of these treasured cookies, I feel like each one is a tasty gift, wrapped in colorful sugars and nonpareils. One December, she came out to the house and spent the night with us. I had made these with her before in her kitchen, but I wanted to spend a little time with her during the Christmas season in my kitchen making a special memory along with a batch of special cookies.

It's a little tricky to get the dough rolled out to just the right thickness, a skill that only time and experience can perfect, so I wanted to really pay attention. I watched and learned as she passed down not only a recipe, but also a tradition. Miss Pat used to get Charlie and his brother, Michael to help with the decorating phase when they were little. With so many cookie cutter options available these days, you can get your family to take part in decorating these delights in their own personal way, and the next thing you know you'll have a tradition of your own.

Charlie likes decorating the tree-shaped ones with brightly colored nonpareils and a cinnamon red hot at the top because it reminds him of the large, glass lights his family had strung around their tree every year. I like the stars and their silver and gold glitter. So, get creative, have fun, and take a moment this Christmas to let food bring your family together. You'll satisfy your sweet tooth and fill your heart with a lot of love. After all, isn't being together with family a big part of what Christmas is all about? I hope you enjoy this recipe for Christmas Sugar Cookies and can get your own family involved in the baking process with you.

Christmas Sugar Cookies

MAKES 3–4 DOZEN COOKIES, DEPENDING ON CUTTER SIZE

½ cup butter, softened

1 cup sugar

1 egg

1 teaspoon vanilla

1½ cups flour

2 teaspoons baking powder

1 egg white, beaten until foamy

Cinnamon Sugar (for dusting each cookie before final decoration)

1. Cream butter, sugar, egg, and vanilla together in a large bowl. Blend flour and baking powder and add to bowl. Mix well, by hand, to form into dough. Cover and refrigerate dough until ready to roll.

2. Separate chilled dough into about 4 or 5 balls. On a smooth, floured surface and with flour on hands, slightly flatten each ball. Flip dough over and slightly flatten the opposite side, incorporating a little bit of flour on each side.

3. With a rolling pin dusted in flour, gently work the dough ball evenly, making sure not to roll over the entire piece more than a couple of times. Work in sections. Roll the sections that are too thick, working from the center out. Dough should be thin, but not too thin as it will be difficult to remove from the surface.

4. Once dough is flat and even in thickness, cut out shapes with a cutter and place on an ungreased baking sheet. Brush each shape with a little egg white. Lightly sprinkle cinnamon sugar on top of each, and then decorate with colored sugars, nonpareils, crushed candy canes, or preferred decoration.

5. Bake at 350° F for about 6 to 8 minutes or until light, golden brown. Remove from tray to a cooling rack. Cookies should be thin and crunchy when cooled.

Nan's Notes: *If the dough gets too thin when rolling or it's sticking to the surface, you can rework the dough into a ball and start over. Make sure there is enough flour on the surface and the rolling pin as well, and the dough is chilled. Practice makes perfect—if you've never rolled dough before, you'll get the feel for it.*

Cookies & Country Music

One of the first questions usually asked of couples is, "How did you meet?" I always say food brings people together. Well, this is the tale of food, music, and dancing that brought two people together!

Before Charlie and I met, he was playing guitar in a country-covers band that toured around the southeast, and I was a singer in a society band. My friend Cindy Rose was in that band with me.

At the same time, my brother Denny and I would frequent a country-dance club in Nashville. The country music dance craze was in full swing at that time, and Denny and I loved to two step…and we were pretty darn good at it if I say so myself! Well, Cindy knew the band that Charlie was playing in needed a couple of dancers for a gig at Good Year Tire and Rubber Company in Akron, Ohio, and she recommended Denny and me. Good Year was fundraising for their United Way campaign and wanted the band to play while dancers pulled some of the workers onto the dance floor to get them engaged. So, with the boot scootin' brother and sister booked as the dancers and Charlie playing in the band, we were bound to meet.

We all met up to leave for Akron at 8:00 a.m., said our sleepy hellos, and climbed into a van for the long drive to Ohio. I had driven all night from a show the night before in Knoxville, Tennessee, and was not feeling too pretty, but Charlie still remembers the moment we met and the flowered dress I was wearing that day. I remember his denim jacket with the suede collar and his blue eyes. Cindy had told me she thought I would like Charlie because he was "so cute and had really pretty eyes." She was right.

Midway into the trip, we made a stop, and when we reloaded into the van, Charlie and I "somehow" ended up sitting beside each other. Mmmhmm. By the time we made it to Akron, he had fallen asleep beside me, and I had rolled his hair with my Velcro rollers. I figured if he was a good sport about that, he had to be alright.

Here is where the food part comes in. The good folks at Good Year put us all up at the Quaker Square Inn. Quaker, as in Quaker Oats! We all made it to our rooms after the long ride to find fresh oatmeal cookies on the pillows. So, Charlie and I continued our conversation with a stroll around Akron, eating our cookies, and falling in love bite by bite. It always comes back to food… one way or another.

Nutmeg Yule Logs

MAKES ABOUT 24–28 COOKIES

This is my favorite Kelley family Christmas cookie. I think about it all year long. I had never had anything like it growing up because my family was more about cakes and pies. When I went to my first Christmas at Miss Pat's house up in Maryland, I got hooked on this flavor. The presentation is just picture perfect, resembling little logs. Put these on a pretty Christmas plate, and let them do their thing.

- ¾ cup sugar
- 1 cup butter, softened
- 2 teaspoons vanilla extract
- 2 teaspoons rum extract
- 1 egg
- 3 cups flour
- 1 teaspoon freshly grated nutmeg
- Nutmeg for sprinkling on top

FROSTING:
- 2¼ cups powdered sugar
- 2 tablespoons butter, melted
- 2 tablespoons milk
- 1 teaspoon rum extract
- ½ teaspoon vanilla extract

1. In a large mixing bowl, combine sugar, butter, vanilla, rum extract, and egg and mix together well with a mixer, until fluffy and airy. Add in the flour and nutmeg and blend well. Separate dough into 6 equal parts.

2. Sprinkle a little flour on a flat surface and with your hands, roll and shape each piece of dough into a long rope. Diameter should be about ½ inch and ends should be rounded off. Slice rope into about 3-inch pieces and place on an ungreased baking sheet. Bake at 350° F for 12 to 15 minutes or until logs are golden brown. Cool on wire racks.

3. In a small bowl, add sugar, butter, milk, and rum and vanilla extracts and mix well. Spread icing on top of each cooled cookie log. Scrape icing with a fork to give a bark-like appearance. Dust each log with nutmeg.

DESSERTS

Peanut Butter Dog Cookies

MAKES ABOUT 20–24 COOKIES, DEPENDING ON CUTTER SIZE

(For Jerry, Olivia, Bailey, Molly, and Chiefy)

We love our dogs, past and present. Since dogs can't speak for themselves, we can only guess how much they like these by their actions. Little Jerry is a jumper and for these, he bumps his head on the ceiling. You can make them just soft enough as well for those senior, dentally challenged dogs like sweet Olivia. She gums the heck out of these!

½ cup hot water (add more water later if needed)

½ cup oil

2 eggs

4 tablespoons natural, crunchy peanut butter

2 teaspoons vanilla extract

2 cups flour

½ cup cornmeal

½ cup old-fashioned oats

1. In a small bowl, blend wet ingredients together.

2. In a large bowl, whisk together dry ingredients, make a well in the bottom of the bowl, and pour in wet mixture. Blend well to form a ball of dough.

3. Preheat oven to 400° F. Roll out dough on a floured surface to about ¼-inch thick. Cut with desired cutter shape and place on a non-stick cookie sheet or lightly greased one. Bake for 20 minutes. When done, turn off the oven and leave dog cookies in the oven as it cools. Cookies will harden. Store in an airtight container.

Nan's Notes: *Our sweet Boxer, Molly was allergic to wheat, so I used rice flour instead of wheat flour, and they turned out great. They longer you leave the tray in the cooling oven, the harder they will get, so remove earlier if you want the cookies to be on the softer side.*

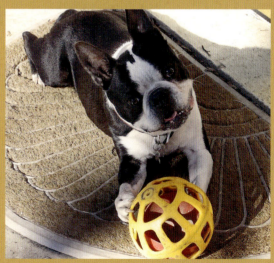

DESSERTS 213

Prune Cake

1½ cups of sugar
1 cup of Wesson oil (any cooking vegetable oil)
3 eggs
2 cups of plain flour
½ cup of buttermilk
1 tsp. each of salt, soda, vanilla, all spice, nutmeg, cinnamon
1 cup of mashed prunes
1 cup of nuts

mix and bake 40 to 45 min.

Sauce

melt 1 stick of
1 cup sugar
½ stick butter

Shrimp Creole

cook ½ c. onions, ½ celery and 1 clove garlic in 3 T oil well tender, not brown. Add 1 #1 can tomatoes, 1 8 oz can tomato sauce, 1 t. salt, 1 t. sugar, 2 t. T. flour

Cranberry Sauce

Never stir this sauce.
One pound cranberries, 1½ c. sugar, 1 pint water.
Put cranberries and cold water on fire in a heavy deep sauce pan. Simmer until berries start popping. Add sugar carefully and continue ...
... in open iron about 20 m...

1 cup dark C. Syrup
½ t. salt
1 t. vanilla
½ c. butter

mix and put in unbaked shell

Fried Apples

6 or 8 cooking apples
1 C. sugar
1 tablespoon ...
... iron skillet ... are clear gummy ...

Carrot Cake

2 cups Plain Flour
2 cups Sugar
2 Tablespoons Cinnamon
1½ Teaspoons Soda
1 Teaspoon Salt
1¼ cups Wesson oil
4 Eggs

... ingredients well ... (loosely)

Vanilla Wafer Cake

cream 1 stick butter + marg + 2 cups sugar
1 lb Vanilla Wafers
2 can coconut
add 6 eggs 1 at a time
then add vanilla crumbs + ½ cup
alternate then 2 cups chopped ...

Index

A

Almond:
    Amaretto Bread Pudding 175
    Baked Apple Pancake 47
    KK's Chicken Casserole 152
    Maple Syrup Strata 56
    Overnight Coffee Cake 55
    Raspberry Chocolate Tarts 178
    Sesame Cabbage Salad 69
Amaretto Bread Pudding 175
Appetizers: *See also* Dips & Spreads
    Bruschetta 30
    Cheese Puffs 27
    Cranberry & Brie Stuffed Mushrooms 33
    Gorgonzola & Pear Puffs 29
    Mexican Wontons 24
    Mixed Nuts Sauté 32
    Nixie's Cheese Straws 26
    Olive Cheese Bites 23
    Pesto & Brie Stuffed Mushrooms 34
Apple:
    Baked Apple Pancake 47
    German Apple Cake 200
Armiger, Katie 148–149
    Chicken with Pesto Cream Sauce 149
Artichoke Soup, Oyster 81
Arugula Salad, Watermelon 65
Asparagus:
    Chicken with Pesto Cream Sauce 149
    Mushroom-Stuffed Ravioli Sauté 131

B

Bacon:
    Bacon, Tomato & Mushroom Dip 21
    Bean Chowder 93
    BLT Pasta Salad 68
    BLT Pizza 105
    BLT Soup 87
    Creamy Cajun Corn & Shrimp with Bacon 116
    Egg Muffins 38
    Gloria's Red Beans & Rice 114
    Miss Pat's Open-Faced Tomato Sandwich 74
    Miss Pat's Spaghetti Sauce 130
    One Pan Chicken & Greens 158
    Potato & Bacon Chowder 92
Balsamic Glaze 30
Banana:
    Banana Split Cake 198
    Brown Sugar Banana Sauce 182
    Fruit Compote 168
Basil:
    BLT Pasta Salad 68
    BLT Pizza 105
    Bruschetta 30
    Chicken Parmesan Lasagna 140
    Fresh Tomato & Basil Pie 48
    Grilled Cheese & Herb Pizza 107
    Italian Vegetable Soup 78
    Margherita Pizza 104
    Miss Pat's Open-Faced Tomato Sandwich 74
    Pasta Con Verdure Fresche (Pasta with Fresh Vegetables) 110
    Pesto 35
Beans:
    Bean Chowder 93
    Cilantro Salmon with Corn & Black Bean Salad 70
    Dutch Chicken 153
    Edamame & Lentils 75
    Gloria's Red Beans & Rice 114
    Gloria's Vegetable Beef Soup 80
    Green Chile Chili 98
    Hoppin' John 112
    KK's Chili 97
    Meatball Soup 85
    One Pan Tex-Mex Pasta 137
    Sausage Bean Soup 76
    Southwestern Sirloin Stew 100
    Southwest Taco Soup 84
    Thyme & Shallots Chicken 147
    Vegetarian Chili 99

Beef:
　Chipped Beef Dip 20
　Eggplant Casserole 109
　Gloria's Vegetable Beef Soup 80
　KK's Chili 97
　Meatball Soup 85
　Meat Loaf Wellington 129
　Miss Pat's Spaghetti Sauce 130
　One Pan Beef Stroganoff 136
　One Pan Tex-Mex Pasta 137
　Slow Cooker Pot Roast 127
　Southwestern Sirloin Stew 100
　Southwest Taco Soup 84
　Sweet & Sour Beef with Vegetables 133
Black, Cindy 174–175
　Amaretto Bread Pudding 175
Blueberry:
　Fresh Berries with Brown Sugar Cream 169
　July 4th Berry Tart 181
Bok Choy:
　Chef Mark Rubin's Rice Noodles Sichuan with Shrimp 120
Bread, Cinnamon Swirl 51
Bread Pudding:
　Amaretto Bread Pudding 175
　Charlie's Chocolate Bread Pudding 173
Brie:
　Cranberry & Brie Stuffed Mushrooms 33
　Pesto & Brie Stuffed Mushrooms 34
Broccoli Cheese Soup, Not-So-Typical 90
Bruschetta 30

C

Cabbage:
　Italian Vegetable Soup 78
　Paprika Potatoes & Sausage Soup 77
　Sesame Cabbage Salad 69
Cakes: *See also* Coffee Cake
　Banana Split Cake 198
　Cheesecake Cup with Cookie Crumble 177
　German Apple Cake 200
　Limoncello Pound Cake 193
　Nannie Broome's Sour Cream Pound Cake 190
　Orange Frisco Cake 189
　Slow Cooker Cake 194
Carrots:
　Italian Vegetable Soup 78
　Orange Rosemary Chicken 163
　Slow Cooker Pot Roast 127

Casseroles:
　Breakfast Casserole 44
　Chicken Casserole 154
　Eggplant Casserole 109
　KK's Chicken Casserole 152
　Maple Syrup Strata 56
　Pecan French Toast Casserole 58
　Potato Sausage Casserole 42
　Shrimp Casserole 123
　Spicy Shrimp Casserole 122
Cheese: *See also* Brie, Feta
　Blue Cheese Tomato Soup 82
　Cheese Puffs 27
　Gorgonzola & Pear Puffs 29
　Nixie's Cheese Straws 26
　Not-So-Typical Broccoli Cheese Soup 90
　Pimento Cheese 73
Cheesecake Cup with Cookie Crumble 177
Chicken:
　Chicken Casserole 154
　Chicken in a Basket 142
　Chicken Jambalaya 144
　Chicken Parmesan Lasagna 140
　Chicken Stroganoff 138
　Chicken with Pesto Cream Sauce 149
　Dutch Chicken 153
　Fennel Chicken Stew 101
　Green Chile Chili 98
　Green Curry Chicken 150
　KK's Chicken Casserole 152
　Margherita Pizza 104
　One Crust Chicken Pot Pie 156
　One Pan Chicken & Greens 158
　Orange Rosemary Chicken 163
　Thyme & Shallots Chicken 147
Chili:
　Green Chile Chili 98
　KK's Chili 97
　Vegetarian Chili 99
Chocolate:
　Charlie's Chocolate Bread Pudding 173
　Kelley Family Chocolate Pie 187
　Peanut Butter & Chocolate Chip Scones 60
　Raspberry Chocolate Tarts 178
　Seven Layer Bars 202
　Slow Cooker Cake 194
Chowder:
　Bean Chowder 93
　Potato & Bacon Chowder 92

Cilantro & Yogurt Dressing 71
Cinnamon:
    Cinnamon Swirl Bread 51
    Nutmeg & Cinnamon Puffs 50
Cobbler:
    Firehouse Cobbler 185
    Grace Ann's Peach Cobbler 183
Coconut:
    Green Curry Chicken 150
    Seven Layer Bars 202
Coffee Cake:
    Overnight Coffee Cake 55
    Sour Cream Coffee Cake 52
Compote, Fruit 168
Cookies:
    Christmas Sugar Cookies 208
    Cornmeal Cookies 203
    Nutmeg Yule Logs 211
    Peanut Butter Dog Cookies 212
    Seven Layer Bars 202
    Spiced Ginger Cookies 201
    Spiced Tea Cookies 204
Corn:
    Cilantro Salmon with Corn & Black Bean Salad 70
    Creamy Cajun Corn & Shrimp with Bacon 116
    Dutch Chicken 153
    Gloria's Vegetable Beef Soup 80
    One Pan Tex-Mex Pasta 137
    Potato & Bacon Chowder 92
    Southwestern Sirloin Stew 100
    Southwest Taco Soup 84
Corn Dodgers 97
Cornmeal Cookies 203
Crab:
    Shrimp Casserole 123
Cranberry:
    Cranberry & Brie Stuffed Mushrooms 33
    Cranberry Scones 59
Creole, South Mississippi Shrimp 124
Crescent Rolls:
    Chicken in a Basket 142
    Gorgonzola & Pear Puffs 29
    Grace Ann's Peach Cobbler 183
    Meat Loaf Wellington 129
Curry Chicken, Green 150

D
Davis, Linda 156–157
    One Crust Chicken Pot Pie 156
Desserts: *See also* Bread Pudding, Cakes, Cobblers, Cookies, Pies
    Brown Sugar Banana Sauce 182
    Cheesecake Cup with Cookie Crumble 177
    Creamy Grape Parfait 171
    Fresh Berries with Brown Sugar Cream 169
    Fruit Compote 168
    Red Wine Strawberry Sauce 182
Dips & Spreads:
    Bacon, Tomato & Mushroom Dip 21
    Chipped Beef Dip 20
    Cream Cheese Shrimp Ball 18
    Creamy Pumpkin Dip 22
    Pimento Cheese 73

E
Edamame & Lentils 75
Eggplant:
    Eggplant Casserole 109
    Vegetable Lasagna 165
Eggs:
    Baked Apple Pancake 47
    Breakfast Casserole 44
    Country Ham Quiche 43
    Egg Muffins 38
    Maple Syrup Strata 56
    Miss Pat's Creamed Eggs 41
    Pecan French Toast Casserole 58
English Muffins:
    Miss Pat's Creamed Eggs 41
    Miss Pat's Open-Faced Tomato Sandwich 74
Evans, Cody 154

F
Fennel Chicken Stew 101
Feta:
    Bruschetta 30
    Grilled Cheese & Herb Pizza 107
    Spinach & Feta Bake 108
    Watermelon Arugula Salad 65
French Toast:
    Maple Syrup Strata 56
    Pecan French Toast Casserole 58

Fruit:
    Firehouse Cobbler 185
    Fresh Berries with Brown Sugar Cream 169
    Fruit Compote 168
    July 4th Berry Tart 181

G

Ginger Cookies, Spiced 201
Grape Parfait, Creamy 171
Greens, One Pan Chicken & 158
Gumbo, Turkey & Sausage 94

H

Halibut, Sweet & Sour 119
Ham:
    Breakfast Casserole 44
    Country Ham Quiche 43
Hoppin' John 112
Howard, David 162–163
    Orange Rosemary Chicken 163

I

Ice Cream:
    Brown Sugar Banana Sauce 182
    Red Wine Strawberry Sauce 182

J

Jambalaya, Chicken 144

L

Lambert, Chef Walter 43
    Country Ham Quiche 43
Lane, Jay 128–129
    Meat Loaf Wellington 129
Lasagna:
    Chicken Parmesan Lasagna 140
    Vegetable Lasagna 165
Leeks:
    Fennel Chicken Stew 101
Lemon:
    Cornmeal Cookies 203
    Limoncello Pound Cake 193
Lentils, Edamame & 75
Lime:
    Cheesecake Cup with Cookie Crumble 177
    Cilantro Salmon with Corn & Black Bean Salad 70

M

Manicotti, Italian Sausage 134
Meatball Soup 85
Meat Loaf Wellington 129

Muffins, Egg 38
Mushroom:
    Bacon, Tomato & Mushroom Dip 21
    Chicken in a Basket 142
    Chicken Stroganoff 138
    Cranberry & Brie Stuffed Mushrooms 33
    Egg Muffins 38
    Fennel Chicken Stew 101
    Miss Pat's Spaghetti Sauce 130
    Mushroom-Stuffed Ravioli Sauté 131
    One Pan Beef Stroganoff 136
    Pasta Con Verdure Fresche (Pasta with Fresh Vegetables) 110
    Pesto & Brie Stuffed Mushrooms 34
    Shrimp Casserole 123

N

Nashville Fire Station 29: 154–155, 184–185
    Chicken Casserole 154
    Firehouse Cobbler 185
Noodles: *See also* Pasta
    Chef Mark Rubin's Rice Noodles Sichuan with Shrimp 120
    One Pan Beef Stroganoff 136
    Sesame Cabbage Salad 69
    Sweet & Sour Beef with Vegetables 133
Nuts: *See also* Almonds, Pecans, Walnuts
    Cinnamon Swirl Bread 51
    German Apple Cake 200
    Mixed Nuts Sauté 32
    Overnight Coffee Cake 55
    Pesto 35

O

Okra:
    Gloria's Vegetable Beef Soup 80
    Turkey & Sausage Gumbo 94
Olive Cheese Bites 23
O'Neal, Jamie 138–139
    Chicken Stroganoff 138
Orange:
    Fruit Compote 168
    Mandarin Orange Salad 66
    Orange Frisco Cake 189
    Orange Rosemary Chicken 163
Oyster Artichoke Soup 81

P

Pancake, Baked Apple 47
Parfait, Creamy Grape 171

Pasta: *See also* Lasagna, Noodles
    BLT Pasta Salad 68
    Gloria's Vegetable Beef Soup 80
    Italian Sausage Manicotti 134
    Mushroom-Stuffed Ravioli Sauté 131
    One Pan Tex-Mex Pasta 137
    Pasta Con Verdure Fresche (Pasta with Fresh Vegetables) 110
    Sweet & Sour Beef with Vegetables 133
Peach:
    Fruit Compote 168
    Grace Ann's Peach Cobbler 183
Peanut Butter:
    Peanut Butter & Chocolate Chip Scones 60
    Peanut Butter Dog Cookies 212
Pear:
    Gorgonzola & Pear Puffs 29
    Mushroom-Stuffed Ravioli Sauté 131
Peas:
    Chef Mark Rubin's Rice Noodles Sichuan with Shrimp 120
    Chicken in a Basket 142
    Fennel Chicken Stew 101
    Gloria's Vegetable Beef Soup 80
    Green Curry Chicken 150
    Hoppin' John 112
Pecans:
    Banana Split Cake 198
    Creamy Grape Parfait 171
    Pecan French Toast Casserole 58
    Pimento Cheese 73
    Seven Layer Bars 202
    Sour Cream Coffee Cake 52
    Strawberry & Pineapple Congealed Salad 67
Pesto:
    Chicken with Pesto Cream Sauce 149
    Meatball Soup 85
    Pesto & Brie Stuffed Mushrooms 34
    Pesto (Homemade) 35
Pies:
    Fresh Tomato & Basil Pie 48
    Kelley Family Chocolate Pie 187
    One Crust Chicken Pot Pie 156
Pimento Cheese 73
Pineapple:
    Banana Split Cake 198
    Fruit Compote 168
    Strawberry & Pineapple Congealed Salad 67
    Sweet & Sour Halibut 119

Pizza:
    BLT Pizza 105
    Grilled Cheese & Herb Pizza 107
    Margherita Pizza 104
Polenta:
    Edamame & Lentils 75
Potato:
    Fennel Chicken Stew 101
    Gloria's Vegetable Beef Soup 80
    Orange Rosemary Chicken 163
    Paprika Potatoes & Sausage Soup 77
    Potato & Bacon Chowder 92
    Potato Sausage Casserole 42
    Sausage Bean Soup 76
    Slow Cooker Pot Roast 127
    Thyme & Shallots Chicken 147
Prosciutto:
    Chicken with Pesto Cream Sauce 149
Puffs:
    Cheese Puffs 27
    Gorgonzola & Pear Puffs 29
    Nutmeg & Cinnamon Puffs 50
Pumpkin Dip, Creamy 22

Q

Quiche, Country Ham 43

R

Ramen:
    Sesame Cabbage Salad 69
Raspberry:
    Fresh Berries with Brown Sugar Cream 169
    Raspberry Chocolate Tarts 178
    Strawberry & Pineapple Congealed Salad 67
Reichart, Selita 140–141
    Chicken Parmesan Lasagna 140
Rice:
    Chicken Jambalaya 144
    Chicken Stroganoff 138
    Gloria's Red Beans & Rice 114
    Green Curry Chicken 150
    Hoppin' John 112
    Italian Vegetable Soup 78
    One Pan Chicken & Greens 158
    Shrimp Casserole 123
    South Mississippi Shrimp Creole 124
    Spicy Shrimp Casserole 122
    Turkey & Sausage Gumbo 94

Rubin, Chef Mark 120–121
    Chef Mark Rubin's Rice Noodles Sichuan with Shrimp 120

S

Salads:
    BLT Pasta Salad 68
    Cilantro Salmon with Corn & Black Bean Salad 70
    Mandarin Orange Salad 66
    Sesame Cabbage Salad 69
    Strawberry & Pineapple Congealed Salad 67
    Watermelon Arugula Salad 65
Salmon with Corn & Black Bean Salad, Cilantro 70
Sandwiches:
    Miss Pat's Open-Faced Tomato Sandwich 74
    Pimento Cheese 73
Sauces:
    Brown Sugar Banana Sauce 182
    Miss Pat's Spaghetti Sauce 130
    Red Wine Strawberry Sauce 182
Sausage:
    Breakfast Casserole 44
    Chicken Jambalaya 144
    Gloria's Red Beans & Rice 114
    Hoppin' John 112
    Italian Sausage Manicotti 134
    Mexican Wontons 24
    Mushroom-Stuffed Ravioli Sauté 131
    Paprika Potatoes & Sausage Soup 77
    Potato Sausage Casserole 42
    Sausage Bean Soup 76
    Turkey & Sausage Gumbo 94
Scones:
    Cranberry Scones 59
    Peanut Butter & Chocolate Chip Scones 60
Seafood: *See also* Shrimp
    Cilantro Salmon with Corn & Black Bean Salad 70
    Sweet & Sour Halibut 119
Sesame Cabbage Salad 69
Shrimp:
    Chef Mark Rubin's Rice Noodles Sichuan with Shrimp 120
    Cream Cheese Shrimp Ball 18
    Creamy Cajun Corn & Shrimp with Bacon 116
    Shrimp Casserole 123
    South Mississippi Shrimp Creole 124
    Spicy Shrimp Casserole 122
Sichuan with Shrimp, Chef Mark Rubin's Rice Noodles 120
Soup: *See also* Chowder
    BLT Soup 87
    Blue Cheese Tomato Soup 82
    Gloria's Vegetable Beef Soup 80
    Italian Vegetable Soup 78
    Meatball Soup 85
    Not-So-Typical Broccoli Cheese Soup 90
    Oyster Artichoke Soup 81
    Paprika Potatoes & Sausage Soup 77
    Sausage Bean Soup 76
    Southwest Taco Soup 84
Southwestern:
    Egg Muffins, Tex-Mex Version 38
    Green Chile Chili 98
    Mexican Wontons 24
    One Pan Tex-Mex Pasta 137
    Southwestern Sirloin Stew 100
    Southwest Taco Soup 84
Spaghetti Sauce, Miss Pat's 130
Spinach:
    BLT Pasta Salad 68
    Meatball Soup 85
    Pasta Con Verdure Fresche (Pasta with Fresh Vegetables) 110
    Spinach & Feta Bake 108
    Vegetable Lasagna 165
Squash:
    Pasta Con Verdure Fresche (Pasta with Fresh Vegetables) 110
Stew:
    Fennel Chicken Stew 101
    Southwestern Sirloin Stew 100
St. John, Robert 144–145
    Chicken Jambalaya 144
Strawberry:
    Cheesecake Cup with Cookie Crumble 177
    Fruit Compote 168
    July 4th Berry Tart 181
    Red Wine Strawberry Sauce 182
    Strawberry & Pineapple Congealed Salad 67
Stroganoff:
    Chicken Stroganoff 138
    One Pan Beef Stroganoff 136

T

Tarts:
    July 4th Berry Tart 181
    Raspberry Chocolate Tarts 178
Tomatoes:
    Bacon, Tomato & Mushroom Dip 21
    BLT Pasta Salad 68
    BLT Pizza 105
    BLT Soup 87
    Blue Cheese Tomato Soup 82
    Bruschetta 30
    Chicken Parmesan Lasagna 140
    Creamy Cajun Corn & Shrimp with Bacon 116
    Edamame & Lentils 75
    Eggplant Casserole 109
    Fresh Tomato & Basil Pie 48
    Gloria's Red Beans & Rice 114
    Gloria's Vegetable Beef Soup 80
    Grilled Cheese & Herb Pizza 107
    Italian Sausage Manicotti 134
    Italian Vegetable Soup 78
    KK's Chili 97
    Margherita Pizza 104
    Miss Pat's Open-Faced Tomato Sandwich 74
    Miss Pat's Spaghetti Sauce 130
    One Pan Chicken & Greens 158
    One Pan Tex-Mex Pasta 137
    Paprika Potatoes & Sausage Soup 77
    Pasta Con Verdure Fresche (Pasta with Fresh Vegetables) 110
    Sausage Bean Soup 76
    South Mississippi Shrimp Creole 124
    Southwestern Sirloin Stew 100
    Southwest Taco Soup 84
    Sweet & Sour Beef with Vegetables 133
    Turkey & Sausage Gumbo 94
    Vegetable Lasagna 165
    Vegetarian Chili 99
Tomlinson, David 154–155
    Chicken Casserole 154
Tortellini:
    BLT Pasta Salad 68
Townsend, Tracy 154–155, 185
Turkey & Sausage Gumbo 94
Turnip:
    Bean Chowder 93

V

Vegetable:
    Gloria's Vegetable Beef Soup 80
    Italian Vegetable Soup 78
    One Crust Chicken Pot Pie 156
    Orange Rosemary Chicken 163
    Pasta Con Verdure Fresche (Pasta with Fresh Vegetables) 110
    Sweet & Sour Beef with Vegetables 133
    Vegetable Lasagna 165
Vegetarian Chili 99
Venier, Victoria 111

W

Walnuts:
    Gorgonzola & Pear Puffs 29
    Orange Frisco Cake 189
    Watermelon Arugula Salad 65
Watermelon Arugula Salad 65
White, Bubba 154
Wine:
    Blue Cheese Tomato Soup 82
    Brown Sugar Banana Sauce 182
    Chef Mark Rubin's Rice Noodles Sichuan with Shrimp 120
    Chicken Stroganoff 138
    Fennel Chicken Stew 101
    Mushroom-Stuffed Ravioli Sauté 131
    One Pan Beef Stroganoff 136
    Potato & Bacon Chowder 92
    Red Wine Strawberry Sauce 182
    Slow Cooker Pot Roast 127
Wontons, Mexican 24

Z

Zucchini:
    Italian Vegetable Soup 78
    Pasta Con Verdure Fresche (Pasta with Fresh Vegetables) 110
    Vegetable Lasagna 165

About the Author

Born and raised in Hattiesburg, Mississippi, southern hospitality and the ability to shoot the breeze with anyone about anything were not just taught—they were practically encoded in Nan Kelley's DNA. "I grew up in a beauty shop, and you certainly pick up the gift of gab around the shampoo bowl," admits Kelley.

The former Miss Mississippi has become a major personality on the Scripps-owned television network, Great American Country (GAC) through her longtime position as host of the popular *Top 20 Countdown*. In addition, she was the host of *Opry Live* for 8 years and has hosted many specials for the network, including the *Academy of Country Music* and the *CMA Red Carpet* shows. Nan has also appeared on the Travel Channel, HGTV, DIY, Fine Living, and the Armed Forces Network.

Whether she's interviewing superstars and legends backstage at the Grand Ole Opry, chatting it up with a fan she meets on the street, or talking through a television screen to a few million folks, Nan has an uncanny ability to connect with people. With her most recent venture, One Pan Nan, she connects with people through food. In this new book of recipes and stories, Nan relates what food meant to her growing up and what it still means today.

When she's not on the road or in the studio, Nan and her husband Charlie, a Grammy-nominated musician/producer, spend time at home in Nashville, Tennessee, with their two dogs, Jerry Lee and Olivia.